"We know that God intends to change how we think and how we behave, but we don't always expect that God intends to change how we feel. But, as *Teach Me to Feel* so beautifully shows, God has given us a whole book—the Psalms—to guide us into feeling rightly. With profound insights tucked into short chapters, Courtney's book helps us apply the words of the psalmists to our own souls—leading us into honesty with God, confidence in God, and joy with God."

NANCY GUTHRIE, Author, *The Wisdom of God: Seeing Jesus in the Psalms and Wisdom Books* and *Even Better Than Eden*

"A good book will teach you about biblical truths, but a great book will lead you to know and love Christ and his word more deeply. *Teach Me to Feel* does just that. Chapter after chapter, I found myself reading the Psalms in a fresh way."

SARAH WALTON, Author, *Hope When It Hurts* and *Together Through the Storms*

"The church has had a rich and right return to the study of God's word and the value of a transformed mind in recent years, but God also gave his people emotions and feelings. How does one navigate feelings faithfully in the midst of suffering, transition, or hurt? Courtney walks us through the Psalms and her own story. She is less a teacher and more a friend on the journey."

LORE FERGUSON WILBERT, Author, *Handle with Care*

"How gracious God is to include in his word a book of songs that gives us the language we need to express the emotions we feel! Courtney Reissig encourages us to slow down and feel, with the psalmists, the realities of life in our broken world. Each reflection helped me to see and savour the goodness of God."

CAROLYN LACEY, Woodgreen Evangelical Church, Worcester, UK; Speaker and Author

"We are told that 'emotional intelligence' is essential. But can we rely on it? Courtney presents us with the richest possible source from which to manage our feelings—the Psalms. Whether praising God or challenging sin, each chapter is a balm for the soul. I would have happily worked through another dozen psalms with Courtney!"

LENI-JO MCMILLAN, Women's Network and Training, City Bible Forum, Perth, Australia

"I love the Psalms, and Courtney Reissig has made me cherish them even more. She shows us how to honestly process our feelings with God, using psalms to express our deepest emotions. If you've ever felt misunderstood, lonely, or overwhelmed and wondered how to biblically process your feelings, this book is for you. You'll discover how to lament, find hope, and rejoice through all of life, drawing you closer to the God of all comfort."

VANEETHA RENDALL RISNER, Author, *The Scars That Have Shaped Me*

"This book comforted, encouraged, and taught me so much. It had the rare quality of making me reach for my Bible, and I read each chapter with the Psalms open alongside. Courtney Reissig gives us keen insights learned through her own personal suffering, so her words are poetic and laden with meaning, yet grounded in reality."

LINDA ALLCOCK, The Globe Church, London

"If we're honest, most of us would admit that few aspects of our lives can seem as chaotic and unpredictable as our emotions. Courtney Reissig, a gifted and wise writer, shows us how the Psalms can help us to take our feelings before the throne of God, and how to see them reordered by the ongoing life of Christ. This book can change your thinking and your feelings for the better."

RUSSELL MOORE, President, The Ethics and Religious Liberty Commission of the Southern Baptist Convention

"I've always had a difficult relationship with my emotions. I have suppressed them in shame, or I have let them loose with reckless abandon. Neither approach has served me well. This is why I so appreciate this book. Through her own wrestle with emotions, Courtney points us to the place where the Lord taught her how to feel them well and wisely—the Psalms. I found great comfort in her words and the insight she brings to these ancient songs. There's nothing like a friend—modern or ancient—to tell us, 'I've been there too.'"

LAUREN CHANDLER, Songwriter; Author, *Steadfast Love* and *Goodbye to Goodbyes*

COURTNEY REISSIG

Teach me to Feel

thegoodbook
COMPANY

To my sons: Luke, Zach, Seth, and Ben

We walked through the valley of the shadow of death and felt His nearness every step of the way.

May you come to call Him good all of your days.

Teach Me to Feel
© Courtney Reissig, 2020

Published by:
The Good Book Company

thegoodbook.com | www.thegoodbook.co.uk
thegoodbook.com.au | thegoodbook.co.nz | thegoodbook.co.in

ISBN: 9781784984441 | Printed in Turkey

Design by André Parker

CONTENTS

HOW I LEARNED TO FEEL

(OR, MEDITATIONS IN
A HOSPITAL BED)

I've always been a feeler. From a very early age, I experienced the highest of highs and the lowest of lows (think Anne Shirley from *Anne of Green Gables*).

But in the space of a single month, my emotions went from the children's roundabout at the theme park of life to the tallest rollercoaster imaginable.

Pregnancy has always brought out my worst fears. I have a history of miscarriages and infertility, so I am well aware that seeing those pink lines doesn't mean a happy ending at the labor and delivery unit. Instead, for me pregnancy is a months-long battle with intense anxiety.

So when I found myself pregnant with our fourth child, I was nervous. And when I began experiencing all the familiar signs of miscarriage, I was certain: *I am losing a baby—again.*

But God had other plans for this boy; so instead of a blank ultrasound screen, we saw a heartbeat. And my fears began to abate. *Maybe we will get to keep this baby after all,* I thought. I scheduled my c-section and began to settle into the final stages of my last pregnancy—I was in the homestretch of the anxiety and started to look beyond it.

And then it all changed.

I JUST WANTED US TO LIVE

When I was 33 weeks pregnant, my placenta partially abrupted. If you aren't familiar with obstetrics (as I was not), this is life-threatening for both the mom and the baby. It is rare, random, and completely terrifying. In a matter of hours, my entire life was turned upside down. If I had feelings, I didn't know how to express them. My emotions often came out in a jumbled mix of anger, terror, grief, and occasional hope. I just wanted my baby to live. I just wanted me to live.

For reasons only known to God, the placenta stopped abrupting, which bought my son three more weeks of time in my womb. But it also bought me a stay in the high-risk unit in the hospital.

I used to think hospital bed rest would be like a mini-vacation. You would get to nap when you wanted. Your food was prepared for you every day. And you never had to clean.

It was nothing like that.

And still the feelings flooded me.

One moment I would feel hopeful. An evening of calm from all the monitors meant we just might be ok. I would feel peace—but it would slip through my fingers. By the next morning, they would be prepping me for an emergency delivery. Then things would stabilize, putting us back in the waiting game. More fear. More anxiety. More confusion. More questions. I couldn't focus on anything of substance for more than a moment, because in a moment everything could change.

When things were hard, my husband, Daniel, and I sat in silence, fearing that just speaking our feelings out loud meant they actually would come true.

In the end, Ben was born. He was ok. But I was not.

When we came home, the feelings only intensified. Sure, we were safe. A stranger on the street would have said we were one, big happy family. But if you go through trauma, you don't get to just come home to the old normal. You have to find a new one. That was the hard task before us. What does normal look like when you now know that life can be snuffed out in an instant? I was grateful, but scared. Sobered, but relieved. I was joyful, yet weepy. I was a walking paradox.

I needed to learn how to feel.

BETWEEN SUPPRESSION AND DIRECTION

Many of us Christian women—in times of crisis, but in normal life too—aren't sure what to do with our feelings. We struggle to know how to feel "Christianly."

So, often, we are prone to suppress our emotions, worried that we are being ungodly. It's the idea that "Christians should feel like this…" and "Christians definitely should not feel like *this*…" So we don't tell anyone how we feel, we hardly admit it to ourselves, and we certainly won't take it to God. We have no idea what to do with fear, anger, envy, and so on… so we try to ignore them and hope they go away.

On the other hand, many of us are much more in tune with our feelings—and much better at expressing them. But then there is the opposite danger, of being so directed by our feelings that how we feel directs what we believe about God and ourselves. We are always up and down. If the wheels fall off, then our faith falls apart.

We need to learn how to feel Christianly. And, though I hardly realized it at the time, in that month on the roller-coaster, I found my teacher. I found the psalms.

A LANGUAGE FOR MY FEELINGS

In the hospital, and in the many months after, the Psalms were my lifeline. Everything else felt meaningless. Everything else was too heavy and exhausting. The Psalms gave me words. The Psalms were, as some have called it, "a mirror into my soul." The Psalms got me, in all my raw emotion over the possibility of losing my son and my own life. They got my joy and my pain. They got my praise and my tears. They understood me when I didn't understand myself.

In the Psalms, I wasn't only understood, but I also had language for my fears. In the Psalms, I had language for my distress. But in the Psalms, I also had language for God—I saw him for who he is, and I was able to trust him. The Psalms sustained me in my darkest moments. The Psalms became as necessary to my health as the hospital-prepared tray that was delivered to me three times a day. The Psalms taught me to feel the reality of life, in all its complexities, and they brought healing in the process.

For three weeks, the Psalms were pretty much the only thing I read. So when the moment came for delivery, I hoped they would sustain me. If it all went south quickly, at least I had been storing up the word—I prayed I could cash in on the deposits.

But in the moment I needed it most, I couldn't remember anything.

My mind went blank. I couldn't remember a single psalm. Not a word. I panicked.

Where was the hope? Where was the life-sustaining truth of God's word that I was banking on?

As they wheeled me into the operating room on the day of Ben's birth, I forgot every single thing.

Except Psalm 23.

As they prepped me for surgery, line after line came to mind:

> *Even though I walk through the valley of the shadow*
> *of death, I will fear no evil.*

As they looked again for Ben's heartbeat…

For you are with me.

As they worked hard to get him out...

Your rod and your staff, they comfort me.

As we heard his first cry coming from lungs that worked...

*Surely goodness and mercy shall follow me all the
days of my life, and I will dwell in the house of the
LORD forever.*

He lived. I lived. As the doctor pulled our screaming baby
from my body, all I could do was weep. I trembled over
the fragility of life—it could be gone in an instant. But I
also rejoiced—death was not the final word that day. And,
looking back, I am grateful that God brought to mind the
psalm that my heart most needed. I needed a psalm—I
needed that one. God knew what I was feeling, which in
that moment was overwhelming fear, and he brought a
word for that fear. That psalm gave me language, and that
psalm shaped my feelings.

CREATED TO FEEL

In this book, I want us to walk together through our feelings, asking God, through the psalms, to teach us to feel—
to see that we have permission to feel, to see that he gives
us language for our feelings, and to understand how God
shapes us in our feelings.

Unlike the narrative parts of the Bible, the Psalms speak
into a static time in Israel's history—the narrative of God's
work among his people is not advanced in the Psalms. Instead, we get a behind-the-scenes look at the mental pro-
cesses and emotions of real people in that story. The Psalms
are the backstory of the biblical narratives, which we may
or may not be familiar with (the stories of Israel's history,

David, and other kings). Instead of providing new details, they slow us down and tell us how God's people are to feel about the stories happening all around them. Old Testament scholar, Derek Kidner, says that the Psalms are intended to "touch and kindle us rather than simply address us" (*Kidner Classic Commentaries, Psalms 1 – 72*, page 42). In the Psalms we get real feelings about real life in this beautiful yet broken world. So if you struggle with knowing how to feel rightly—how to process your feelings instead of suppressing them or being directed by them—and want to know how your feelings can grow your faith, this book is for you. The Psalms are speaking to you.

In the Psalms, we meet people just like us—weak, scared, tired, and hopeless at times; and at other times content, grateful, and praising. In the Psalms, we see stories like ours and feelings like ours. But in the Psalms, we see the end of the story. We see that God always shows up: not always in the way we expect, but he never leaves us or forsakes us. The Psalms remind us that God is always working, even when he seems absent. That's hopeful for us. That's healing for us.

Of course, the Psalms are not primarily about our feelings; they are first and foremost about God. And this book is not any kind of full insight into the Psalms. But the Psalms are poetry, and so they are meant to make us feel something. God's word should make us think, but God's word should also make us feel—and feel deeply. Mark Futato says that, "Since God feels and you are created in God's image, feelings are part of your human experience" (*Joy Comes in the Morning*, page 60).

I surely won't be able to cover every feeling you may be experiencing right now, far less every emotion you will one day experience—but I hope you will find words for your pain or sorrow, joy or praise. By seeing a particular feeling displayed in a particular psalm, you will be inviting God to teach you to feel. You will be letting him give you language to cry out to him or praise him, giving you a way to grow in your faith and through your feelings. God cares about every part of his image-bearers—including our feelings.

The best way to read this book is slowly, and prayerfully! And it's good to start with Chapters 1 and 2, focusing on Psalms 1 and 2, first. These psalms set the context for the entire book of Psalms—they are a prologue of sorts to the book and will help you understand what the rest of the psalms are doing. Then, from chapters 3 to 23, you can plot your own route through, depending on where you are in life right now. But I'd encourage you not to only read about the feelings you are walking with right now—because, if we have lived any time at all, we know that tomorrow things can change, and it's good to learn how to feel well ahead of time. Then chapter 24 is the conclusion.

At the end of each chapter I have included some additional psalms, if you would like to dig further into the way the psalms help you with that particular feeling. Some chapters will have more "extras" than others, because some of the feelings are addressed more frequently in the psalms. Some of the psalms I point you to will be darker than the one we focused on in the chapter, and some will be lighter—drawing you out of darkness, towards hope. Again, remember the truths of Psalms 1 and 2 as you read!

I don't know where you are at today with your feelings. But I do know this: that those feelings can lead you to appreciate your Lord and Savior more, and help you grow in your faith. More than anything, I hope you will see that God hasn't left you, that he cares for you, and that he is ready to meet you in the Psalms.

HAPPY IS THE WOMAN WHO... PSALM 1

Blessed is the one ...
whose delight is in the law of the LORD,
and who meditates on his law day and night.

Psalm 1 v 1-2 (NIV)

Have you ever had a recurring dream where you walk into a situation completely unprepared? Maybe you find yourself in a classroom and you forgot to study for the test. Or you have a big presentation to give and you forgot to change out of your pajamas.

I have such a dream before every big or out-of-the-ordinary thing I do. When I was a waitress, I would dream that I was the only waitress in the entire restaurant on a busy Saturday night. When I travel, I dream that I miss my flight or forget my luggage. When I was pregnant, I would dream that the baby came and we weren't ready (that dream came true in real life each time). When I'm supposed to get up early to run with a friend, I dream that I miss my alarm and wake up to the sunlight.

Can you tell that I don't like being unprepared?

I want to tell you a story about two women and their preparedness.

The first woman is a new mom, and like many new moms she is overwhelmed. Her transition to having small children is proving harder than she expected. She has less time than ever before. She is more tired than she had thought possible. She is overwhelmed.

And she doesn't read her Bible anymore.

It's not that she has stopped following Christ. It's that life has seemed too hard and too complicated since having a baby. What began in the chaos of the first days after childbirth has become practice out of habit. She just doesn't read God's word.

Her husband tries to encourage her to find pockets of time for Bible-reading during naptime or when the baby goes to bed at night. But she just can't bring herself to do it. It's been too long. It's not familiar to her anymore. It's lost its luster. So she fills her days with other things, like social media and television, in the vain hope that she might be able to will herself out of her new-parent exhaustion.

She once promised herself that she would never become like those other women who abandoned the word when their babies were born—but pride goes before a fall, and now she is one of those women: alone, empty, and trying to fix her situation apart from God and his word.

She wouldn't admit it, but her lack of time in the word shows. Her relationships suffer. Her marriage suffers. Even her mothering suffers. Her feelings are all over the place, and everyone (including her) bears the brunt of them. As she looks at what her life has become, she realizes she is woefully unprepared for her new life as a mother.

Let me tell you about another woman not too far away from this new mom. She has been in this same place before: exhausted, overwhelmed, and unable to find a new routine.

But she has emerged with a new purpose. She has seen the bitter fruit that comes from not meditating on God and has vowed to avoid that situation again at all costs. God has been faithful, even in the midst of great difficulty. God has made his word her delight, in the scary moments before her son's birth and in the exhausting newborn days. Meditating on the word doesn't change the difficulty of her days, but it does give her perspective. It keeps her grounded in her relationships. It gives her strength for her role as a mother. It gives her hope. Her circumstances are not dissimilar to those of the first woman, but what she is doing with God's word in those circumstances has made all the difference.

Life isn't necessarily easier for her than for the first woman. But this woman is prepared for the hurricane of difficulty, because she has a weighty anchor.

You guessed it. Each of these women is me.

My early days of motherhood were not my finest moments. I didn't read my Bible for six months—and it was obvious by my every word and action. But as you have read in the Introduction, that wasn't the final word in my life. God is faithful to his people, and he brought me back around. And in my moments of great distress, God showed up through his word. I still remember those days in the hospital, waiting for Ben to be born, anxious about the outcome for his life and mine. In those days, God's word was so sweet to me, not because it removed the difficulty or the fear but because in those very moments of my distress I had the promises of God staring me in the face as I read the words on the page, and imprinted in my mind as I recalled them through the day and night.

In other words, I had learned from experience that Psalm 1 is true.

Psalm 1 tells us where the blessed (the Hebrew word for "happy") life is to be found. This theme of being "happy/

blessed" will come up again and again in the psalm, and in this book. But blessedness is not our usual notion of happiness—the feeling produced when everything works out in our favor. Instead, it is a happiness rooted in something outside of us. The happy life the psalmist experiences is rooted in God, his word, and his purposes. The same is true for us.

And blessing is found in meditating on God's word day and night (Psalm 1 v 1-2). If one of the purposes of the Psalms is to give us language for our emotional responses to life's difficulties and successes and drive us back to God, then to start by talking about God's word makes perfect sense. The Psalms begin with the value of the word (the Bible) because God wants us to be prepared for what is to come.

PREPARE BY DOING SOMETHING NOW

Many people (rightly) think of laments when they think of the Psalms. The Psalms are filled with a lot of sadness and difficulty (which we will talk about soon). How do you prepare for things like physical suffering, injustice, envy, your friend disowning you, depression, or even feeling that God has left you?

You start with the Bible.

But on the flipside, the Psalms are also filled with testimonies of God's faithfulness, of prayers answered, and of deliverances accomplished. How do you respond to the joys, successes, triumphs, and answered prayers of life without boasting in your own strength?

You start with the Bible.

The best way to prepare for such seasons is to start now. This is why Psalm 1 tells us that the blessed man or woman makes God's word his or her meditation day and night. Do you want to live a blessed life, a happy life? Know God through his word. The first step to preparing for the waves of suffering that break upon all of us at some point is to lay the foundation of God's word in your soul. The first step to preparing for the highpoints in life is to lay the foundation of God's word in your soul. If you don't want to abandon him in despair in your greatest distress or turn from him in self-reliance in your greatest triumph, you're going to need the word.

THE RESULT OF YOUR PREPARATION

Sometimes it can seem that I am reading my Bible and getting nowhere. Sometimes it seems that I am reading my Bible and it is not doing anything in my soul. Sometimes, as I said in the Introduction, I read my Bible and forget everything I have read. But God has promised to work through his word, so we can trust that even if we don't feel like he is working, he is.

The psalmist says that spending time in God's word does something for the believer. The Christian who is rooted in the word will be like a fruitful tree that doesn't wither and die (v 3-4).

I live in a part of the US where pine trees are everywhere. When a tornado comes through town, the pine trees are devastated. The needles are all blown off, and then the trees themselves fall to the ground. Why don't they stand? Because their roots are shallow. But do you know what kind of tree isn't leveled when a tornado comes through town? Hardwood trees. They have deeper, stronger roots—and they stand firm.

This is the type of tree that the psalmist has in view. A hardwood tree starts small, in seed form, but over time (sometimes a very, very long time) it grows. It starts with the roots. The roots are planted, firm and deep, and cannot be moved. And then flowers bud on the branches, and leaves grow, and then it's a tall, mature tree. But this is a process. It takes time. It doesn't happen overnight. But it is steady. It is secure. It is rooted and grounded and cannot be moved—not by storms, not by tornadoes, not by floods. Its roots dig deep. Sometimes in our town a hardwood tree grows right next to a pine tree, and they can look equally sturdy when all is going well—but the truth is in the roots. The hardwood stands firm, like the one who is rooted in God's word.

Like the hardwood tree, the woman who delights in God's word, meditating on it day and night, will prosper in the fiercest storm and in the favor of spring. You are nourished deep in your roots by the streams of water that you are planted near. This is the fruit of God's word in your life. It's a process. It takes work. It takes time. But it will happen. This is the image we need to keep in mind as we look at how the Psalms speaks to our emotions. The woman who is able to stand in times of lament is the one rooted in God's word—she is like a hardwood tree. This doesn't remove the difficulty of life or even take away the deep feelings we have (as we will see in other psalms), but it does give us a foundation to fall back on. We may feel as if we are being torn limb from limb, but if we are rooted in God's word, we still stay standing.

When the tornado comes, the tree's roots are a matter of life and death. And so it is for us. Psalm 1 talks of living and dying (v 5-6). There is a lot of contrast in the psalm between the wicked and the righteous. The wicked die, and they will have no leg to stand on in the judgment to come. The righteous prosper and grow because they are rooted deeply in the word. The wicked, verse 4 says, are like "chaff." Why? Because chaff has no weight and no root. It's the leftover from wheat, separated out in the winnowing process and lying on the threshing floor. Chaff is useless. It is waste. It has nothing grounding it, and it will blow away on even the smallest gust of wind.

I get that. This is how I felt when I didn't make God's word my delight.

But contrast that with the one who meditates on God's word. The one who meditates on God's word doesn't perish, failing to stand in the tornado of God's judgment (v 5-6). The one who trusts in God lives. What an incredibly hopeful truth as we walk right into the great emotional ups and downs to come in the Psalms, and in our lives! Death may be around us, and one day will be right before us, but we know the end from the beginning.

Blessed is the woman who makes God's word her delight: who meditates on it day and night. In all that she does she prospers (v 3). The prosperity that the psalmist is talking about is not having all your prayers answered in the way you want—having a full bank account or even lots of friends. It's a prosperity of a different kind. It's a prosperity of fruitfulness; it's a prosperity of sustaining grace in difficulty; it's a prosperity of holiness as you spend time in the word; and, most importantly, it's a prosperity of life everlasting. Amazingly, this prosperity is something that doesn't end but only grows forever and ever (John 4 v 14). The prosperity that this life offers is temporary and fleeting. But the prosperity that the psalmist is talking about can't be ripped from you even in death.

ONE MESSAGE, ONE BOOK

This is the message all throughout the Psalms. Knowing the end from the beginning sustains us all throughout the middle. We will see this again and again throughout this book.

This is the message not just of the Psalms, but all throughout the Bible. Think for a moment about what the New Testament says about Jesus. He is the Word made flesh in John 1. He is, as *The Jesus Storybook Bible* puts it, everything that God reveals about himself, in a person. Jesus loved the word. Jesus taught the word. Jesus fulfilled the word. And Jesus is revealed to us in the word. The Bible has no category for loving Jesus but not loving his word.

Jesus embodied Psalm 1. He was prepared for the darkest suffering, and he was prepared for the greatest joys, because he knew and delighted in God's word. He quoted from the psalms because he knew the psalms and saw his life in light of the psalms. So if we love Jesus, we will love the psalms; and if we love the psalms, we will grow in our love for Jesus. In the next chapter we will look at Psalm 2, which talks more about Jesus specifically, and helps set up the whole psalter (along with Psalm 1). It talks about a promised king and the Son of God. It will help us fix our eyes on Jesus' certain victory and prepare ourselves for the hardships and joys of life.

This is what it means to be prepared. You know the end from the beginning, so you have hope in the middle. And you know the way of blessing, so you're ready for the tornadoes as well as the sunshine. The Psalms can only be understood in light of Psalm 1. Each, as we meditate on it, will strengthen and secure your roots as you take up its water. You won't understand lament, suffering, sorrow, repentance, or any other thing that comes your way if you don't first see that God's word has to be your delight. You won't have language to cry out to God in your suffering if you don't let him teach you through his word.

If you are reading this in the midst of great suffering, and sense that you don't have a strong foundation in God's word, it is not too late. It's never too late. This is why I wrote this book. You could start in the Psalms today and find sustaining hope even if God's word hasn't been your foundation up until now. Even if you are coming into this book unprepared for the suffering that you are enduring, God hasn't left you and is able to meet you in the pages of the Psalms.

Blessed is the woman who treasures God's word. She will find she is able to stand, even in adversity. She will know what it is to be blessed, even in difficulty. And she will not perish.

Journaling

_____

_____

_____

_____

_____

_____

_____

_____

_____

_____

_____

_____

_____

_____

_____

_____

_____

_____

_____

_____

_____

_____

A KING AND A KINGDOM
PSALM 2

I have set my King on Zion.

Psalm 2 v 6

I'm an Olympics enthusiast. In fact, I'm slightly obsessed. When the Olympics are happening, I guard my news intake like a toddler guarding a snack from his hungry little brother. I do not want spoilers. I do not want anyone taking Olympic joy and surprise from me.

Of all the sports the Olympics feature, swimming is my absolute favorite. I study the swimmers' form. I watch every single heat, every single race, and every single human-interest story. I have my favorite events (the 50m freestyle and the individual medley). I have been known to print out the swimming schedule, lest I miss a favorite event.

So you can imagine my dismay when I turned on the nightly news during the 2012 Summer Olympics to hear these words during the opening credits:

"Ryan Lochte beats Michael Phelps in the 400m individual medley."

Did I mention I hate to hear spoilers during the Olympics?!

The event had not even been televised in America until that point, but there I was, sitting in front of my television, trusting the news anchor to protect me from spoilers; but oh, no, he couldn't hold the news in. It was the race I had been waiting for in the weeks leading up to the Olympics, and with one sentence from an evening news anchor the surprise was gone. Sure, the race would be fun to watch, but it wouldn't be the same. I knew who had won—now I was just watching to see how he had won. I'm still recovering from the disappointment.

I do *not* like spoilers.

But there is a kind of spoiler that I make an exception for. It's actually the spoiler of a lifetime: one that we all need as we walk through this broken world. It's this (don't look away now): *Jesus wins and he will reign forever.*

We see it right here in verse 6 of Psalm 2:

> *I have installed my king*
> *on Zion, my holy mountain. (CSB)*

In many ways, the message of the entire Bible is captured in this one sentence. God has crowned a king, his name is Jesus, and his kingdom will know no end. Psalm 2 is setting the stage for the entire book by giving us the final outcome first. It's preparing us for what is to come in the psalms by preparing us for what is to come once and for all through the perfect king.

This is not just any king; this is God's king, the Lord's king. But there is more. He is not a temporary king. He is a forever king.

Psalm 2 was a coronation song for the kings of Israel—for the monarchs who were supposed to call God's people to trust him, follow his word, and look to him to rule over them forever (Genesis 49 v 10; Deuteronomy 17 v 14-20). It is a royal psalm for the king. But... there is a problem here. Look at verses 8-9 of Psalm 2:

Ask of me, and I will make the nations your heritage,
and the ends of the earth your possession.
You shall break them with a rod of iron
and dash them in pieces like a potter's vessel.

This king is not just the king over Israel—he is the king over the nations, and he is the judge of the nations. Yet even the greatest king of Israel, David, never got beyond the eastern Mediterranean—so how can any king of Israel be described as ruling and reigning over ends of the earth? The psalm must either have sounded like a joke—especially since the kings after David ruled over a broken and shrinking kingdom—or it was a promise: of a future king far greater than David—a king who would put an end to the raging and plotting of the nations of the earth (v 1). Psalm 2 shows us the world as it was and is (nations conspiring against God and his plans), but it also has a spoiler. There is a king who wins. In that day, he was yet to come. In ours, that king is already seated on his throne, and there is a day in the future when his rule will be recognized all over the earth, and all the conspiracies and rebellions will cease. Jesus wins and he will reign forever.

Psalm 2 spills the beans as the book of Psalms starts. It shows us God's purposes for all time at the beginning. But there is a reason for that. Psalm 2, like Psalm 1, sets up the book of Psalms. If you know that a life rooted in the word leads to life and blessing, then you have hope when it doesn't feel like you are being blessed. Equally, if you know that Jesus wins and his kingdom will reign forever, then you are sustained when enemies and suffering surround you on every side and it feels like he won't win. You need the spoiler, or you won't make it when life gets hard.

HOW DOES IT PREPARE US?

Most people don't go to the psalms to get encouragement about the end times. Instead, we often go to the psalms for encouragement when our here-and-now is proving to be hard. And for good reason. The psalms often deal with really hard times, when it appears that King Jesus is not winning. In fact, Psalm 3 (the very next psalm) immediately takes us to a time when the king was not winning. Psalm 3 is "a psalm of David, when he fled from Absalom." Absalom was David's son; he mounted an insurrection against his father, took over David's kingdom, took David's fighting men, and even tried to take David's wives (2 Samuel 13 – 19). David, the rightful king, had to flee from his own son and his own city. In Psalm 3 he is under attack, and looks to be out of options.

That's life. It's harder more often than it's easier—and it has the capacity to shock us with what goes wrong. But Psalm 2 helps us in that it shows us God's certain plan. Whatever happens, this remains true:

> *As for me, I have set my King*
> *on Zion, my holy hill. (v 6)*

The lesson of Psalm 1 is, *You need God's word.* The take-home of Psalm 2 comes in verses 11-12:

> *Serve the LORD with fear,*
> *and rejoice with trembling.*
> *Kiss the Son,*
> *lest he be angry, and you perish in the way,*
> *for his wrath is quickly kindled.*
> *Blessed are all who take refuge in him.*

God enthroned his anointed king at the death, resurrection, and ascension of Jesus. While it might look (and feel) like the anointed king is not ruling currently, we know by faith and for certain that he is sitting at the Father's right hand right now and forevermore (Romans 8 v 34; Colossians 3 v 1; Ephesians 1 v 20). This anointed Son is the One we are to serve with fear, to rejoice over with trembling, and to kiss in honor and worship. Just as we are blessed by our consistent meditation on the word, we are also blessed by our complete devotion to the Son, God's anointed King. We are to joyfully and tremblingly serve him, both in the present and the future:

> *Being found in human form, [Jesus] humbled himself by becoming obedient to the point of death, even death on a cross. Therefore God has highly exalted him and bestowed on him the name that is above every name, so that at the name of Jesus every knee should bow, in heaven and on earth and under the earth, and every tongue confess that Jesus Christ is Lord, to the glory of God the Father.*
> *(Philippians 2 v 9-11)*

Doesn't that sound like Psalm 2 v 6? This anointed Son is now exalted; he is above every name. There was a time when it did not look as if he was winning—no one looked at him on trial before Pilate, or carrying his cross to Golgotha, and saw a victorious king. And yet, he now sits at the right hand of the throne in heaven. The anointed king reigns forever. The promise has been fulfilled and will one day be completed at his second coming.

REFUGE WHEN THE WORLD RAGES

So, if you know the end and you know who wins, what do you do? You kiss the Son. You humble yourself in submission to the king. You cling to Jesus.

This realization—that the promised king of Psalm 2 is as living and active as the psalm presents him—is an encouragement to weary Christians who are trying to make sense of their broken and sorrowful earthly lives. The nations might be raging, the people may be plotting, but one day God's king will put all of his enemies under his feet for good. Until then, kiss the Son, trust the king, and rejoice in his omnipotent reign. You will be blessed—you will be happy.

Psalm 2 tells us that there is and will be a king—whatever anyone says or does. So the rest of the psalms teach us how to drive through life with Christ's enthronement seen in our rearview mirror and the final victory of Christ appearing ahead through our windshield. We just have to drive through the storms of life to get to that final destination—the heavenly kingdom.

As we will see throughout this book, there are some really heavy storms ahead. There are going to be seasons of life when you lament, and others when you praise, and others when you're not sure what to do. You need Psalm 2 because of what is waiting for you in the psalms after Psalm 2: for all the complexity of life—despair, darkness, praise, joy—is there.

So, remember Psalms 1 and 2 as we move on. In Psalms 1 and 2 you have been shown God's purposes (this is what we were made for). All throughout the psalms you will see fall and redemption, in the psalms of lament and thanksgiving. And then in the final psalms, we'll reach restoration (this is what we hope for). There are psalms of lament mixed in with psalms of praise because that is the kind of life we live. We are sorrowful, yet always rejoicing (2 Corinthians 6 v 10). In the psalms and in life, we need Psalm 2's spoiler fixed in our hearts. One Psalms scholar, Mark Futato, says:

> *"One purpose of the Psalms was and is to create a sense of hope that one day the King would come to put everything in our lives and in the world in right*

order once and for all. We're going to find out that
the Psalms create an expectation that the King is
coming." (*Transformed by Praise: The Purpose*
and Message of the Psalms, page 131)

Psalm 2 helps us towards that end. As we read the remaining psalms, especially the ones filled with deep questions and suffering, we need this perspective in view. The king is coming, and he will one day make everything right. The king has come, and he has not forgotten his subjects. The king is our refuge (v 12).

Psalm 1 tells us how to flourish both now and forever—meditate on the word and get life. Psalm 2 gives us a grid for viewing the future and a hope to anchor our lives on—Jesus wins and he will reign forever.

So however your life is going and whatever you're facing right now, if you're trusting Jesus as your King, you have already made the most important and best decision you ever could. Your life will never fail to have purpose and hope, and your destination is utterly secure: not because of you, but because of him. Jesus wins.

This is a good and important word as we get ready to enjoy the psalms. Psalms 1 and 2 tell us where to place our hope, even when it feels as if what has been promised isn't happening for us right now. Psalms 1 and 2 give us a foundation to stand on, so that when the storms of life come, we have a refuge from the storm.

Jesus wins and he will reign forever. That's a spoiler worth hearing again and again. Find your refuge in him.

Journaling

LET DOWN
PSALM 55

For it is not an enemy who taunts me—
then I could bear it;
it is not an adversary who deals insolently
with me—
then I could hide from him.
But it is you, a man, my equal,
my companion, my familiar friend.

Psalm 55 v 12-13

There are few things more isolating than the feeling that a friend has betrayed you. You used to spend hours sharing life together. You enjoyed one another's company. You had fellowship together around your shared faith. You vacationed together. You watched each other's kids. But now it's all gone. Now the friend you once knew as dear and faithful is distant and cold. To make it all worse, you are beginning to think your ex-friend is now actively against you. You hear whispers of slander, lies, and hurtful words, but you don't know who knows what or even who your friends are anymore. You have lost a close friend and are fearful of losing more.

Feeling let down in this way is almost too much to bear emotionally, or even physically. It messes with your head, which messes with your body. It is all-consuming, exhausting, anxiety-inducing; it's just plain awful.

This is how David felt as he penned Psalm 55. Distress was not an unfamiliar feeling for him. Many of the psalms were written by David, and many were written under pressure.

Psalm 55 is a psalm of lament. While many of the psalms have praise as their key theme, over half are actually lament psalms. Like the psalmist, we often have to work through a lot of difficulty to get to the point of praise.

WHAT IS A LAMENT?

We are unfamiliar with lament in our current culture. In our churches we tend towards happy songs and phrases, rather than the sad, melancholy tone of lament psalms. But lament is part of the Bible and should be part of the Christian life. (For a more detailed take on lament, read *Dark Clouds, Deep Mercy* by Mark Vroegop.)

Lament psalms follow a general structure:

1. Cry to God for help
2. Complaint of circumstance/trouble
3. Trust in God's work and deliverance
4. Praise for God's deliverance

And in Psalm 55, David's lament is for a lost friend and over a painful betrayal. He's been let down, and badly.

DAVID'S FRIEND PROBLEM

> *Give ear to my prayer, O God,*
> *and hide not yourself from my plea for mercy!*
> *Attend to me, and answer me;*
> *I am restless in my complaint and I moan,*
> *because of the noise of the enemy,*
> *because of the oppression of the wicked.*

> *For they drop trouble upon me,*
> *and in anger they bear a grudge against me.*
>
> *(v 1-3)*

In verse 4, David says he is "in anguish." In verse 5, he says "fear and trembling" have come upon me. He has enemies and oppression on every side. He feels forgotten and betrayed by those who are against him. But verses 12-13 tell us the primary problem that David is enduring. It is not a general relational difficulty with general enemies. No, this is personal. This is betrayal, at its core, for his feelings have been caused by one who used to be his dear friend. And it is utterly debilitating.

We get further explanation of what this betrayal involves in verses 20-21:

> *My companion stretched out his hand against*
> *his friends;*
> * he violated his covenant.*
> *His speech was smooth as butter,*
> * yet war was in his heart;*
> *his words were softer than oil,*
> * yet they were drawn swords.*

Words are a sneaky business. They can bring life, and they can bring death, sometimes in the same sentence. They can be masked as hope but lay a smack down of discouragement. And the one who knows how to use words the best has the power both to wound and to heal, and tends to do both (I know this as one who has done both). David is experiencing the truth we all know—that the familiar phrase "Sticks and stones may break my bones but words will never hurt me" is utterly false. And it's worse when the hurtful words come from the mouth of a former friend. An enemy might use words to tear their opponent down, but if that enemy is a former friend, the daggers pierce deeper and more permanently. they get at our psyche in ways that only a friend could.

The great nineteenth-century preacher Charles Spurgeon said:

> *"None are such real enemies as false friends. Reproaches from those who have been intimate with us, and trusted by us, cut us to the quick; and they are usually so well acquainted with our peculiar weaknesses that they know how to touch us where we are most sensitive, and to speak so as to do us most damage ... We can bear from Shimei what we cannot bear from Ahithophel."*
> *(The Treasury of David, Volume One, page 446)*

Ahithophel was David's friend and ally, but when the king's son Absalom betrayed David, Ahithophel went with Absalom—leaving David bereft of both his friend and his son (2 Samuel 15). In the next chapter, Shimei hurls curses and stones at David. But Shimei was from the house of Saul (David's enemy)—coming from him, it was a different type of attack: more expected and less painful. This is what Spurgeon is getting at here:

> *"The sly mysterious whisperings of slander often cause a noble mind more fear than open antagonism; we can be brave against an open foe, but cowardly plotting conspiracies bewilder and distract us."*
> *(page 448)*

It is hard to recover from feelings of betrayal. As in many of the psalms of lament, as you read this psalm you see that David is all over the place. He goes from trusting God to crying out to God for what he is enduring, and then back to trusting, and then back to crying again. And isn't that how betrayal works? A dear friend turning his or her back on you leads you to serious doubting. It can lead to depression. It can lead to physical ailments. It can lead to an inability to sleep. It can lead to the desire to sleep all the time because the sadness is too much. It can lead to thoughts that bounce between speaking harshly to yourself and believing the worst of everyone else. It can lead to a craving for escapism.

Do you know how betrayal feels? Maybe you know it right now. And this psalm is telling you: God gets how that feels, and it is ok to feel it.

WHAT ABOUT MY FEELINGS?

It's one thing to be let down by someone you aren't emotionally invested in, but what about the friend you have had since kindergarten? What do you do when she suddenly turns against you? What about the husband? What about the sister or brother in Christ? David is telling us that we should feel something when someone we are close to betrays us. When you have a repository of memories with this person stored up, betrayal will make you feel something. It should make you feel something.

Psalms 1 and 2, as they set up the Psalter, tell us what life should be like and what life will one day be like. We were made for friendship and fellowship. We were made for relationships that last. We were made to treat others with kindness and respect. But here in Psalm 55 there is none of that. Life here is nothing like God intended. It's all back-stabbing and lies. Life in this post-Genesis-3 world is constantly screaming at us that all is not well. This is what led to David's angst. It is what leads to ours as well. We know what is true and right. We know what God intended. But we are regularly met with the exact opposite. And we feel that disjointedness deeply.

HOW DOES PSALM 55 HEAL?

There are some psalms that you can't read without seeing Jesus. And when we think of betrayal by a friend, it's not hard to see how Jesus is the one who faced the worst betrayal of all.

The Psalms are the songbook of God's people and give us a language in our anguish, and Jesus could have sung this one:

> For it is not an enemy who taunts me—
>   then I could bear it;
> it is not an adversary who deals insolently with me—
>   then I could hide from him.
> But it is you, a man, my equal,
>   my companion, my familiar friend.
> We used to take sweet counsel together;
>   within God's house we walked in the throng.
>
> (v 12-14)

Jesus knew how it felt to be betrayed by someone who had called himself a close friend. First, there was Judas, selling Jesus to the highest bidder. Then there was every other disciple, who deserted him as he was arrested; and his very closest friend Peter, who denied even knowing him. In the hour of his greatest need, Jesus was left utterly alone before his accusers. That is betrayal. Have you been let down, badly? You have a Savior who faced that—who tasted that bitterness to the greatest degree. He knows intimately what it feels like when someone you used to "take sweet counsel" with turns their back on you and denies you.

So how do you process the feelings that are unleashed when a friend betrays you? First, you allow yourself to feel those things. Psalm 55 gives you permission to. But then, you need to trust—trust that God will hold you fast even in the aftermath of a friend letting you down. Look at verse 22:

> *Cast your burden on the LORD,*
>   *and he will sustain you;*
> *he will never permit*
>   *the righteous to be moved.*

And this is where Psalms 1 and 2 also teach us how to cope. The blessings of Psalms 1 and 2 are not only going to be true in eternity, but are true now even in the midst of this fallen world. They show us how to live the blessed life even through suffering. The disorientation that brings laments does cause the psalmists to wonder whether or not they are in the path of blessing—but when they are reoriented on God's word and his king, they can rest assured that they are walking that path, even when it doesn't seem like it. They battle through the angst because of what they know to be true of God and his purposes.

Psalm 55 begins and ends with God. While David is incredibly honest and raw about his feelings throughout it, he knows where he can turn with those feelings as they threaten to overwhelm him. You can cast your burden on the Lord because he will sustain you and preserve you. What do you need when you feel betrayed by a close friend? You need something outside of yourself to bear you up, because there is nothing inside us that will sustain us when a "familiar friend" is gone. Psalm 55 feels the betrayal with you. But it also moves you to hope—to throw your burden on the Lord. You don't have to carry it alone. Instead, you can cast this great betrayal on the one who understands and who sustains. Betrayal can make you feel like you have nothing keeping you steady—that this will knock you flat and that there's no getting up or moving on—but verse 22 comforts us by saying that that's not possible for the believer. God will keep you grounded even when your circumstances don't.

IN THE END, TRUST

There are going to be a lot of references to trusting God in this book. While every psalm might be dealing with different circumstances, they all land here eventually. We can too, even if we might wrestle along the way. The psalms are calling us to trust God again and again. They are calling us to trust God when friends betray us. They are calling us to trust God when we can't see what he might be doing. Trust is the end goal for all of us—but sometimes it just might take us a while to get there; and sometimes—as in David's case here in Psalm 55—it might mean we trust, and then go back to crying out, then trust God for a moment, then go back to crying out. But the final goal is that we begin and end with trust—with a lot of feelings all throughout the middle.

David ended where we all must end. David knew God, and because he knew God, he knew that God would deliver him eventually. When you are let down by a familiar friend, when the arrows of slander are thrown at you, or when you feel you can't trust anyone around you anymore, you can trust the one who "redeems [your] soul in safety" (v 18). As the New Testament puts it, you can trust the one who will keep you to the end (Philippians 1 v 6). In the betrayal of a friend you might feel that it has taken everything earthly from you, but that person can't take the most important thing—your soul.

But even as you find hope in this, the feelings remain. Of course they do. Betrayal is hard. There is no getting around that. Like the psalmist in Psalms 1 and 2, we must look to what is to come while we wrestle with the feelings of the present. Your familiar friend may be gone, but there is a friend who sticks closer than a brother (Proverbs 18 v 24). His name is Jesus, and no amount of betrayal can take him from you.

Extra Psalms: Psalms 57, 59, 69

Journaling

_____

_____

_____

_____

_____

_____

_____

_____

_____

_____

_____

_____

_____

_____

_____

_____

_____

_____

_____

_____

_____

DESPAIR
PSALM 88

For my soul is full of troubles,
and my life draws near to Sheol.

Psalm 88 v 3

*"There are years that ask questions and years that
answer."* (Zora Neale Hurston,
Their Eyes Were Watching God)

Have you ever faced the years of questions? Month after
month where it seems you walk in suffering with no
relief, and you wonder when the answer will come. Day after
day you cry out to your family, your friends, anyone who
will listen—begging for answers, but there are none. There
are seasons that lead to questioning everything. Maybe you
are there now. Maybe you have been there for a long time.

I know how you feel. And as you will see in this chapter,
countless people throughout the centuries know how you
feel as well.

After Ben was born, I thought we would come home from
the hospital and just return to life as "normal." I thought we
would bring a baby home alive, bring me home alive, be
reunited with the rest of the family, and just put the painful
hospital chapter behind us.

We didn't. I couldn't.

It was constantly in front of me—taunting me, terrorizing me, and taking every ounce of energy and joy I had left. I thought checking out of the hospital meant leaving that difficult episode behind us, never to be revisited again. I was so very wrong.

We seemed like a happy family on the outside, but inside the darkness raged. Nearly dying and nearly losing your son has a lasting impact. I couldn't just return to normal life because in my mind any semblance of "normal" was gone. I had to learn to live with what I was left with. I was afraid to leave the house. I was afraid to go to sleep. I was afraid to leave my kids in the care of anyone else. I was afraid of dying. I physically felt the pain of my own and my son's mortality, and I had no idea how to return to the world, now that it seemed dark and scary.

I wasn't going back to my mental "normal" and I wasn't going back to my physical "normal" either. With each passing month, my physical difficulties increased too. Recovering from the C-section proved far more difficult than from my previous ones. I kept getting sick. I needed another surgery. For nearly a year and a half, our family was marked by a relentless stream of trials. What began as an isolated instance of suffering became an ongoing pattern of having to face the brokenness of this world again and again and again.

We were drowning. *I* was drowning.

There were days when I couldn't get out of bed because the depression, darkness, and physical pain were more than I felt I could face. I lived with a constant fear of what would happen next. One night I looked at my husband and said, "I feel like God is against me." And I meant it. God didn't appear to be in our corner. The feeling of despair was real and potent. The depression lingered on with no sign of relief. I began to realize that I was going to have to come to terms with a new normal—one I saw in Psalm 88:

You have taken from me friend and neighbor—
darkness is my closest friend. (v 18, NIV)

I did feel as if "darkness [was] my closest friend" and brokenness my constant adversary.

That is where I was. This is where a lot of us are. This is where the psalmist was in Psalm 88. Despair is a common feeling, and God intends to comfort us by reflecting our despair in his word. It's as if God is saying to us, *I know you, and I know your struggles. I'm showing you that you aren't the only one who feels this way.* Your circumstances might look different, but the despair is the same. The origin of despair is as varied as the genetic makeup of every person—a chemical imbalance in the brain, or a relational difficulty, or a change or lack of change in circumstances, or physical suffering, or a combination of all those things. And sometimes, there is no explanation for it. Psalm 88 is for us when we are in that place, when the darkness doesn't seem to let up and instead weighs heavy on us, like a wet blanket in the dead of winter. The psalm is generic enough in its expression of despair that Christians of all personalities and situations can find hope in its words. Whatever the darkness we are walking in, and however long we have walked in it, Psalm 88 is given to us in that darkness.

This is a lament psalm, which follows a certain pattern—a cry to God, a complaint about circumstance, a turning point of trust, and then praise for deliverance. Except you will find something noticeably absent in this particular lament psalm. There is no turning point of trust. It ends in darkness.

Psalm 88 carries all the marks of a typical lament psalm, like Psalm 55 and others—and then all of a sudden it doesn't. It moves all through the feelings of despair that come from physical suffering, relational suffering, and even depression—and then there is no "but." It is dark and sad and doesn't find a resolution quickly—or, in fact, at all. Many call Psalm 88 the darkest psalm in the Psalter, and for good reason. Just look at how it ends:

You have caused my beloved and my friend to shun me;
my companions have become darkness. (v 18)

The end.

And yet I find this psalm—one of deep, unresolved sorrow—comforting. Life isn't tidy. Within this life, our circumstances don't always resolve in a neat and hope-filled ending. Sometimes, like the psalmist, we spend years or even our entire lifetime afflicted and depressed (v 15). And there are some days when we can't see how God is working or even muster the faith to trust him. Like the man in Mark 9 v 24 whose son had an illness that raised questions to which there had been no answers, we need God to help our unbelief—but sometimes we don't even have the words to pray those words.

Whenever I talk about the psalms, I almost always mention Psalm 88. I'm often surprised how few people know much about it. I think some of that is owing to the fact that it scares us. We don't know what to do with a person who doesn't tack on an expression of trust and praise at the end of lament and complaint, especially when it comes from holy Scripture. But it is holy Scripture. It is inspired by God. It is there to instruct us and encourage us, so we must deal with it. But even more than that, I know there are many Christians who, one way or another, live in this psalm daily (I am one of them), so to ignore its rich truths is to neglect the provision of hope for weary Christians. We need Psalm 88.

GODLY, YET STRUGGLING

First, we need to get some context for the psalm. Its author, Heman the Ezrahite, is likely the same Heman mentioned in 1 Kings 4 v 31 as being not as wise as Solomon (so, still wise, but not the wisest man ever). Since the fear of the Lord is the beginning of wisdom (Proverbs 9 v 10), Heman was godly as well as wise—and he was in the depths of despair. He feels lonely (Psalm 88 v 8). He feels hopeless (v 18). He feels afraid and anxious (v 3). He feels unheard (v 9-12). He wonders if God cares for him. He feels that his friends have left him in his suffering.

A testament to Heman's wisdom lives permanently in Scripture. Evidence of his godliness lives in the Psalms. This isn't the kind of person we expect to have a seeming crisis of faith. But doesn't knowing that a wise, godly believer wrote this, and felt like this, comfort you if you feel similar despair? The truth is, Christ-loving believers despair. It's not a sign of lack of faith. This is vital to remember again and again and again. Your despair is not a commentary on your faith or standing before the Lord.

We know Heman feels despair, but he also feels something else. He feels certain about God's sovereignty over his suffering. After recounting the magnitude of his despair, he makes clear that he knows who is responsible. It's God:

> *You have put me in the depths of the pit,*
> *in the regions dark and deep.*
> *Your wrath lies heavy upon me,*
> *and you overwhelm me with all your waves. Selah.*
> *You have caused my companions to shun me;*
> *you have made me a horror to them.*
> *I am shut in so that I cannot escape;*
> *my eye grows dim through sorrow. (v 6-9)*

Here is a man who recognizes that all he is enduring comes from the sovereign, unfathomable hand of God. Can't you hear the confusion in his words? *It's you who has done this to me,* he cries. He knows who ultimately did this to him, and it only compounds the grief.

CRYING OUT

And yet knowing that God is sovereign also gives Heman something to cry out in his grief. He cannot change his circumstances, but he can ask God to do that for him. He cries out to him, begging him to change things. This is the hopeful part of Psalm 88, even though it might not seem hopeful at first glance. The only reason Heman can cry out to God is because he knows God, and he knows that God is the only one who can save him (v 1). He might be in the depths of despair and feel like he is being left alone, but he knows where he can turn. He might be completely confused by what God is doing, but because he knows God is in control, he knows he can cry out. So can you.

We will find ourselves going back to this truth again and again in this devotional, because it helps us understand the Psalms and all of the Bible. The psalmist is appealing to what he knows to be true and what he knows to be promised, even when—or especially because—everything around him is telling a different story. Psalm 1 and Psalm 2 tell of what is promised and what is to come. The rest of the psalms tell us about real life and how we respond to it. In verses 10-12 we get this paradox. *Can I praise you when I'm dead?* he asks. *I know who you are, but will I praise you in the grave? What does this say about you?* Psalm 1 tells us about the blessed life that comes from being rooted in the word. Psalm 2 tells us about the king and his kingdom. In Psalm 88 we get none of that. There is no blessing, and there is no prevailing kingdom. So how do you live in light of that? Heman tells us that you appeal to God and what you know about him and what he's promised. *I'm meant to praise you,* he basically says. *But I can't do it when I'm dead. Help me.*

COMFORT IN THE DARKNESS

The key is this: in his darkness, Heman does not stop praying, and he does not stop being honest with God. You might not get relief right now, and there is no real formula for finding relief, but you can still cry to him day and night (v 1, 9, 13). God might not bring relief, but he does always hear (Romans 8 v 26-27; 1 John 5 v 14-15).

Still, the psalm doesn't end with healing. It seems there is nothing to find in it that can offer healing to us in our despair. But I think that's exactly the point. Psalm 88 doesn't give us a prescription for healing our despair because that's impossible. Sometimes in this life healing never comes. Sometimes healing comes after many years. Sometimes healing comes only to return us to the pit months or years later. This darkness isn't tidy or easy to find a solution for, and that's why Psalm 88 is in the Bible—to remind us that we are not alone. Heman the Ezrahite didn't get his relief (that we know of). Unlike other psalms of lament, there is no corresponding psalm of thanksgiving for this one. It just ends with darkness. As strange as this may sound, I find that comforting. I'm not the first or last who will have to sit in darkness for a while. You aren't either.

Before we end this chapter, it's really important to say emphatically that depression isn't sin. We need to say this again and again to those struggling with depression. Sometimes life is just dark, and you see no light. We live in a broken world where all manner of things lead to depression and despair. God did not originally design the world to be full of suffering and sin. This is why Psalm 1 and 2 are always helpful to keep in view, especially as we read

Psalm 88. Psalm 1 and 2 tell us the ideal; Psalm 88 tells us something about the place where we all live while we are waiting for Christ to return and make all things new (Revelation 21 v 5). Until then, even the godliest Christians feel despair or struggle with depression.

When we look at Psalm 88 closely, we see that the resolution might not come, but the cry of desperation is going to the right place—God. It begins with God: "O Lord, God of my salvation, I cry out day and night before you" (v 1); and ends with God: "You have caused my beloved and my friend to shun me" (v 18). It's a dark, despairing psalm of unanswered prayers. But it reminds us that we aren't alone. We aren't the first, and we won't be the last, who have dealt with such despair. And we can keep crying out, for as long as it takes. Praise the Lord for Psalm 88. Zora Neale Hurston was right. There are years that ask questions and years that answer. What a comfort that he provides language for us in the years that ask only questions, and offer no answers.

Extra Psalms: Psalms 77, 102, 143

Note: One of the most helpful books I've read on Christians and depression is a book by David Murray called *Christians Get Depressed Too*. I read it in the height of my struggle with post-partum and post-trauma depression and it was a balm to my soul. If you need comfort and encouragement, I highly recommend this book.

Journaling

FORSAKEN
PSALM 22

My God, my God, why have you forsaken me?

Psalm 22 v 1

There is nothing worse than the feeling that God has forgotten you. There is nothing more terrifying than that experience of looking at your life, asking yourself, "Is he here? Does he hear? Does he care?" and then finding yourself answering, "It seems he doesn't."

Live long enough, and at some point you will feel forgotten, even forsaken, by God. Live long enough, and you will find yourself singing along with the hymnwriter "Though the darkness hide thee, though the eye of sinful men thy glory may not see" ("Holy, Holy, Holy"). Sometimes it's hard to see his holiness, his power, and his goodness. Sometimes all you feel is forgotten and alone.

That is where we find ourselves in Psalm 22. It opens with that familiar and heart-wrenching question—"My God, my God, why have you forsaken me." It's familiar because Jesus cried it when he was in anguish on the cross (more on that later). But don't let its familiarity dull the truth that it's heart-wrenching ("my God") and despairing ("why?"). This is coming from a man—a king, no less—who knows God personally and deeply, which only intensifies the agony of feeling forsaken.

This psalm is simply divided into two clear sections: the cry (v 1-21), and the praise (v 21-31). It falls into a typical pattern for a lament psalm—crying out to the Lord leads to praise for his deliverance. In many ways, it's a lament psalm and a thanksgiving psalm rolled into one.

THE CRY OF THE FORSAKEN

The first section of this psalm tells us what the writer, King David, feels. He feels forsaken (v 1). He feels like God doesn't hear him (v 2). He feels like his prayers are falling on deaf ears and are in vain. He feels scorned and worthless (v 6-8). He feels alone (v 11). He feels like death is near because of his enemies (v 11-14). He feels weak (v 15-18). He is crying out to God repeatedly, and God doesn't seem to be hearing him or answering him.

Have you been there? Are you there now? You feel as if God has given up on you. Psalm 22 is for you, friend. Where do you go? What do you do when you feel forgotten by God? Let David be your guide here.

For me, one of the most helpful things about this psalm is how frequently David goes back and forth between trust and despair. In verses 1-2 he cries out in despair. In verses 3-5 he appeals to God's character and past faithfulness to his people. Then he despairs again, and in verses 6-8 he cries out as he plunges down a spiral of hopelessness. This leads him to remembering God's faithfulness in personal ways in verses 9-10. God has been his God from birth; how can he not trust him now? But that, too, is short-lived, and from verse 12 he is back to seeing only what is happening around him.

Who doesn't vacillate between true and untrue thoughts? You hear words that tell of your worthlessness, and you despair; but then you remember that your worth is in being created in God's image, and you feel a little better; but then your eyes look away for a moment, and you see enemies on every side, and you doubt all over again.

It's the Christian life, isn't it? One step forward in trust and then, very quickly, one step back in distrust. It's frustrating. It's normal. David knew this vacillating; and yet David didn't stay there.

So what did David do with his feelings of divine abandonment? First, he was honest about them. Second, he reminded himself of what is true despite them.

David cries out to God in his despair. He reminds himself of true things about God's past faithfulness to himself and to his people; and he reminds himself of God's character. God is unchanging. He is the same yesterday, today, and tomorrow. What God did for his people in times past, he will do for his people in the future. God's word is unchanging. The promises he makes, he keeps. When we feel we have been forgotten by God, we can do what David did. We can cry out and say, "God, this is how it feels. This is how it looks me, honestly." And we can—we have to—remember what he has done for his people (both in broader history and in our personal history). We can remember who he is. It might not change our feelings immediately, but it didn't change David's either. But it will bear fruit eventually.

Often, when I can't make sense of what God is doing, I pray to him a prayer based on what I know to be true about him. I will say things like "God, I know you care about everything you have made, including me. Will you show me you care here in this confusing circumstance?" I will rehearse in prayer what I know to be true about him: he is good, he is kind, he is gracious, he is loving, he is patient, he has forgiven me, I am united to Christ and have fellowship with the Father. Dark circumstances can cloud the true reality of who we are in relationship with God. Often it requires a degree of intentionality on our part to see that he truly hasn't forsaken us. Sometimes we still can't see that he hasn't forsaken us, but we pray nonetheless. And we wait. Because there is more to say and to know.

GOD SHOWS UP

The space between verse 21 and verse 22 is the clear turning point in this psalm. In verse 21 David is begging God to save him from the mouth of the lion and the horns of the wild oxen (the threat of death and destruction). The Christian Standard Bible translates verse 21 most helpfully (and, according to scholars, accurately):

> *Save me from the lion's mouth,*
> *from the horns of wild oxen.*
> *You answered me!*

And then in verse 22, suddenly David is praising God in the midst of his family. It's almost as if David's in the middle of his despairing cry, with enemies threatening him on every side, and then God breaks through and answers.

Up to this point, David has been going back and forth between his despair and his recollection of God's character towards him. Up to this point, he has heard only silence. And then at the end of verse 21 something changes. God answers him. With a shout of joy, David gets his answer of deliverance, and the entire psalm shifts in tone and language.

Isn't this how God works sometimes? You cry out to him for relief, you pray for a change in circumstances, you recount what he has done to bolster your own faith—and you only get silence. Then one day it all changes. Your heart warms, your faith increases, your prayers are answered.

Psalm 88 reminds us that sometimes we live in darkness and depression for a long time—and Psalm 22 reminds us that sometimes God answers us in the middle of our cry of distress. This is so encouraging. It's a reminder to stay the course in our prayers for deliverance. Persistence in prayer will not return void in your life. It will either remind and reassure you of God's character in the difficulty or it will grant you the relief you are longing for. Appealing to God based on what you know to be true about him is not a futile effort. One day you might just find your prayers have been answered. In eternity, you certainly will.

So what does David do with this answered prayer?

He praises God. In verses 7-8, David tells God that his silence towards him is leading to God's name being mocked. It's not just David who is scorned by the silence—it's God. Those who mock him doubt that God is strong to save in verses 7-8, but from verse 22 onwards they can doubt no longer. All who see David's deliverance see that God has done it. David's personal deliverance is for corporate good (v 22-31). Remember, the word "psalm" literally means "praise." Praise is the point of the psalms, but not every psalm includes praise. This one does, and it encourages us in our own times of feeling forgotten by God. In these moments we can cry out to him honestly, appeal to his character and past faithfulness, and wait. He might just show up when the horns of the proverbial wild oxen are directly over you (v 21). Or you may have to wait. But when he does answer you, praise him as the one who delivers, so that all may see that he has done it (v 31).

JESUS' PSALM

While most psalms are not explicitly referred to by Jesus, in the case of this psalm the New Testament couldn't be any clearer. In fact, many Bible scholars and commentators see this psalm as the most Jesus-focused of all. He directly quoted it on the cross (Matthew 27 v 46). The New Testament tells us that he fulfilled verses from this psalm

(Matthew 27 v 35; John 19 v 24). He brings the nations to himself (Psalm 22 v 27). He is the King who will rule the nations (v 28). The earth will be full of his glory (v 29). His name will be praised forever and ever (v 30-31).

After all, even as we read David's cry, it feels as though this depth of affliction can't be entirely attributed to David, difficult though his life was at times, and forsaken by his God as he felt. So what is he doing? Why does he talk like this? David is speaking prophetically. He is acting as a prophet, speaking of himself but also pointing beyond himself and speaking of what is to come.

Why is this comforting to us when we feel forsaken and forgotten? Because Jesus was actually forsaken by the Father—which is why he cried out as he did. And he was forsaken so that we would never be forsaken. We may feel forsaken sometimes—but his forsakenness was the guarantee that such a feeling of ours will not, cannot, become reality.

Yet this psalm is also Jesus' psalm because he was a human who felt all this agony deeply. To be human in this fallen world is to feel pain. James Johnston says:

> "This is one of the most intimate and personal connections we have with Jesus as he suffered for our sins. The Gospels tell us what happened to Jesus physically; they also give us his seven last words from the cross. But through the prophet David, the Holy Spirit tells us what Jesus was thinking and feeling inside as a human being like us."
>
> (The Psalms: Rejoice the Lord is King, Volume 1, page 234)

On the cross, Jesus was our Savior from the pain, but he was also our model in the pain. As the perfect human, he shows us that it is ok to cry out in this way when we feel forsaken. In fact, I would argue that it is necessary. Cry out to him. Tell him how you feel. Remind him of his character and what you know to be true about him. You have a sympathetic Savior who understands how you feel and gives you language in your agony as well as a future beyond your agony.

That is why the psalm ends with praise: because deliverance has happened. David was delivered from his forsakenness. Jesus was delivered from death in the resurrection. We will one day be delivered as well—maybe in this life, but most certainly in the next. Ralph Davis says this about verse 24:

> *"If Messiah was not finally cast off in his most extreme distress, is it likely we will be in any lesser troubles? If he at last knew God's smile, can't we expect to see the same once more? So the Delivered One passes on this testimony to you: 'He has not despised and he has not detested the affliction of the afflicted'—and you can carry that text into the pit with you."*
> *(Slogging Along in the Paths of Righteousness, page 157)*

This life is not easy. Psalm 22 shows us that we will likely feel forgotten and forsaken by God at times as we walk this hard road to our heavenly home. David felt it; Jesus actually experienced the reality of it. When you feel it, you can and should go to God with those emotions. The Savior did, so you should do no less. And because he was delivered, you will be too. You can take that promise to the bank. When we feel forsaken by God, we can follow David's pattern of persistent prayer, remembering God's faithfulness and character; and then, by his grace, waiting for it to lead to praise and faith in his eternal purposes. And when he delivers us, we can praise him and tell of his deliverance to all who will listen—and of how, looking back, we knew he was there, with us and for us, all along.

Extra Psalms: Psalms 10, 71, 89

Journaling

IN PAIN
PSALM 6

Be gracious to me, O LORD, for I am
languishing;
heal me, O LORD, for my bones are troubled.

Psalm 6 v 2

I once attended church a few days after having surgery, and as I sat in the service that morning, the position of my body made the pain from surgery only intensify. I'd thought I was fine that morning, but sitting like that made me acutely aware that I was not yet anywhere close to fine. I couldn't stand to sing. I couldn't focus on the sermon. I wasn't able to pray. The pain was louder than anything else in the room, and it was debilitating.

As I left church that morning, I had a newfound sympathy for those living with chronic pain. Pain has a way of shutting out everything else and shaking us to our core. It's a near-constant adversary—one that doesn't let anyone else in to provide relief.

Psalm 6 is a psalm that speaks of great pain. David says that his "bones are troubled" (v 2). The CSB translates it as his "bones are shaking." And God is not surprised by that kind of pain; nor does he leave us alone in it.

I've revisited the memory of that Sunday-morning pain (and this psalm) a lot over the years, as life in a broken world has brought pain into my life in various seasons. Pain is so often all-consuming and disorienting. Pain might even make reading this chapter hard. Perhaps you need to read it in short bits because pain inhibits your concentration. It is awful. But God has given us his word for all of life, including this part. Psalm 6 has given me language in my own pain, when all I could do was cry, drenching my bed with tears (v 6), begging for relief. I pray it gives you language in your own.

THERE IS HOPE

This is a psalm of David, but besides that we don't know much about the context of his prayer for relief. This is helpful because it allows us freedom to apply the psalm to a variety of circumstances. Because of the general nature of the psalm, we can find comfort in whatever pain we face. All David tells us is that his suffering is affecting him physically and spiritually (verses 2-3, 5). This is the way of physical pain—it is so debilitating because it affects our emotions and spiritual life too. You can't limit it to "just" your physical nature, because you *feel* pain. Pain is as much an emotional experience as it is a physical one.

Strikingly, this psalm is meant to be sung by God's people. The heading includes multiple references to the musical nature of the poem:

> *To the choirmaster: with stringed instruments;*
> *according to The Sheminith.*

That all seems strange; most of us don't usually sing psalms in our worship gatherings; you probably don't know what "The Sheminith" is (I don't); but most of all, it's hard to imagine singing the specifics of this psalm in a worship service.

When was the last time you sang, "O LORD, rebuke me not in your anger" (v 1)?! Your favorite worship-song lyric is likely not, "I am weary with my moaning; every night I flood my bed with tears" (v 6). But the psalmist expects us to sing the praise and the lament together. The psalmist expects us to pour our hearts out to God in joy and in pain—in worship. It is a hard thing for us to wrap our minds around, especially in a Western context, but this psalm was written for God's people to sing, so it is for us to sing even now as God's people.

The psalms are meant for God's people as much as they were meant for the authors who wrote them. They are meant to encourage, strengthen, instruct, and empathize in the myriad trials, joys, pain, and praise that we experience. So, here in Psalm 6 we have just that—a universal psalm for the universal church. This was to be sung by the choir, leading the congregation: which tells us that the experience of pain is normal, and also that expressing pain to God is necessary. You can cry out to God in worship, just like David in Psalm 6, and it will be beautiful to him. You can lament to God in your pain and be a faithful Christian.

In Psalm 6, David is teaching us to pray. We often think that prayer should be about praising God for who he is and what he's done, and it does include those elements, but prayer is also about desperate people begging God to do what they can't do for themselves. That's what David gets to here right from the outset—verses 1-2 begin a passionate plea for God to remember him and be gracious to him. So David shows us how to feel, he shows us how to worship, and he shows us how to pray, all in this psalm that is filled with great anguish. That's encouraging as we wrestle through pain that doesn't seem to let up. God is guiding us along in our difficulty, because—let's be honest—when pain is ravaging your body, you don't have the energy to figure out what to say or how to worship. Here God says to us, through David, *Let me help you find the words you need.*

PAIN'S SIDE-EFFECTS

The words David finds for his pain and anguish are raw, and they are common when we are overcome with pain:

> *O LORD, rebuke me not in your anger,*
> *nor discipline me in your wrath.*
> *Be gracious to me, O LORD, for I am languishing;*
> *heal me, O LORD, for my bones are troubled.*
> *My soul also is greatly troubled.*
> *But you, O LORD—how long? (v 1-3)*

Pain can make you feel that God is against you. It can even make you feel that God hates you. At the height of our suffering, our mind can play tricks on us—hurling doubt on even the most fervent believers. Psalm 6 is a collective exhalation. Our feelings might not be true, but they are most certainly real. In that raw emotion, we ask, "How long?"

So pain can lead to anxiety and doubting. It can even make you weak or sick. (The Christian Standard Bible translates "troubled" in verse 2 as "weak.") And pain is emotionally draining:

> *I am weary with my moaning;*
> *every night I flood my bed with tears;*
> *I drench my couch with my weeping.*
> *My eye wastes away because of grief;*
> *it grows weak because of all my foes. (v 6-7)*

Pain has some hard side-effects that tend to hang on and drain us of any energy that is left. You get the sense from David that for him, this is a near-constant battle. It is happening all throughout the night. It has gone on for a long time.

MOVING TOWARDS OR DRIVING AWAY

Pain questions what we know and believe, and it doesn't let up. Pain asks many questions but never gives any answers. Pain confuses us. It doesn't let any light in. You wonder when the pain will end, and, like David, you may cry out all night long.

And pain can do one of two things to us.

First, it can either move us towards God in trust because we know God and we know he loves us, despite what the pain suggests:

> *Turn, O Lord, deliver my life;*
> *save me for the sake of your steadfast love. (v 4)*

Or second, it can drive us away from God, causing us to reject him and become hardened against him because of what we see happening in or around us.

As one who has faced severe physical pain for long periods of time over the last few years, I know firsthand that in those moments, you are relying on what you already know to be true to sustain you. When the pain rushes in, you need fuel in the tank to drive you all the way home. Fumes simply won't cut it.

In pain, you will either listen to God, who is sovereign over your pain; or you will listen to the pain that is screaming at you that God can't help or can't be trusted. Pain has a way of grounding you on the path you've chosen. Or to put it another way, pain has a way of refining you and showing you who you really are. It can expose you in your waywardness and draw you back to God, or draw you closer to the God you've been trusting all along—or it can reveal that you never had any sure footing to begin with, like the seed that fell on the thorny and rocky soils in Matthew 13. And so pain is, strangely, an unasked-for opportunity, if we allow it to be, stripping us of what we may hold too dear, moving us back to where we should be, and showing us that our all-sufficient God is the only one worth trusting (Job 23 v 10).

This is how David treats his pain. He can respond in faith because of what he knows about God. He's already on the right path, so when suffering comes, he has the tools necessary to hang on even though it is bumpy. You can respond in this way, too, because of what you know about God. This is why Psalm 1 is utterly crucial to understanding and believing. It really matters what you meditate on. The blessed life is found in knowing God through his word. How else will you stand when your bones are troubled and when you are languishing? How will you flourish like a tree planted by streams of water when it feels as if the water supply has dried up? You meditate on the word, and you stand in adversity—even pain.

But living out of Psalm 1 doesn't mean life is not a struggle. It certainly was for David, as Psalm 6 shows us. First, he cries out to God and appeals to him based on who he is (Psalm 6 v 1-5); then he goes back to weeping and anguish (v 6-7). Lament is a back-and-forth struggle. *Turn and answer me, Lord! I know who you are!* becomes weeping and grief before it becomes confident trust again. This is the pattern of the human experience. We cry out in trust, and then we cry out in anguish, and then we cry out in trust again. Pain is hard and it is real, and there is sometimes a road for us to walk to get to that place of trust. But the road eventually will lead us back to the God who hears, who understands, and who is ready to comfort us in our pain. Knowing him through his word is what gives us the strength to cry out in the way that the seventeenth-century Puritan pastor Richard Sibbes directs:

> *Are you bruised? Be of good comfort, he calls you.*
> *Conceal not your wounds, open all before him and*

take not Satan's counsel. Go to Christ, although trembling as the poor woman who said, 'If I may but touch his garment' (Matthew 9 v 21). We shall be healed and have a gracious answer. Go boldly to God in our flesh; he is flesh of our flesh and bone of our bone for this reason, that we might go boldly to him. Never fear to go to God, since we have such a Mediator with him, who is not only our friend but our brother and husband.

(The Bruised Reed, page 9)

Your Lord is not going to push you beyond what he will also give you the grace to endure. He is not going to look down on you, and he is not going to fail to use your pain. Knowing this is how you get the strength to keep crying out to him in pain. With the cry comes the sustaining grace.

PAIN AND THE HOPE OF THE NEW WORLD

In this psalm, David hasn't received deliverance yet.

Depart from me, all you workers of evil,
for the LORD has heard the sound of my weeping.
The LORD has heard my plea;
the LORD accepts my prayer.
All my enemies shall be ashamed and greatly troubled;
they shall turn back and be put to shame in a moment. (v 8-10)

David says that God has heard him, but do you notice the tense of verse 10? It's in the future. David doesn't say that God has done this to his enemies. He says he will do it to his enemies. David is turning to God in trust before the deliverance comes. How can he do that? Because of what is true in Psalm 2 and all throughout the Bible. Remember, Psalm 2 sets up the Psalter by telling us God's plan for all time—to establish his kingdom forever through his Son, Jesus. One day, every enemy will be defeated—and that gives David hope. One day, this king's king will make all things new—including a pain-filled body. It's this view that encourages us when the pain of life threatens to undo us, as in Psalm 6. It won't last forever.

The future promised to him in Psalm 2 is what enabled David to cry out in faith, even when the deliverance was still far off. The future promised to us in that psalm, in Revelation 21 – 22—where Christ returns and makes all things new—and even all throughout the New Testament enables us to do the same. We have the same confidence that David had in Psalm 6 v 10. All of our enemies will be dealt with one day—even the enemy named "pain." As we wait, we cry out with honest pleas to the only one who can sustain us and heal us, the only one who can redeem our pain by using it and then removing it—the Lord, who reigns over all.

So we cry, "Come, Lord Jesus." And we know that when he does, we will cry no more.

Extra Psalm: Psalm 38

Journaling

_____
_____
_____
_____
_____
_____
_____
_____
_____
_____
_____
_____
_____
_____
_____
_____
_____
_____
_____
_____
_____

WORTHLESS
PSALM 8

When I look at your heavens, the work of
your fingers,
the moon and the stars, which you have set in
place,
what is man that you are mindful of him,
and the son of man that you care for him?

Psalm 8 v 3-4

"I just feel like I failed as a mom," she said to me over coffee. She's not the first and she's not the last woman to feel like a failure. To be honest, it's a refrain I repeat to my husband nearly every day in some variation.

"I am a bad writer."

"I am a bad neighbor."

"I am a bad wife."

"I am a bad friend."

"I am a bad mom."

"I am a bad church member."

I feel worthless.

Sound familiar? The single woman who wants to be married feels worthless because no men seem interested in her. The overworked woman feels worthless because she can't fulfill her work responsibilities and maintain her friendships. The wife feels worthless because she can't connect with her husband anymore. The women's minister feels worthless because there are so many needs and not enough hours in the day to meet those needs. The stay-at-home mom feels worthless because she gave up a promising career to stay home with children who cannot give her feedback on how well she is doing, and she feels like the working world has moved on without her. The working mom feels worthless because of the judgmental voices that tell her that she is losing years with her children.

Popular self-help books tell us that if we just believe in ourselves or speak positively to ourselves we will feel better. But what if you are so far gone that you can't even think of anything good to say about yourself? And even if you're able to talk to yourself in the mirror, the positive feelings don't last long—because when what we accomplish, what we give up, what we do, and what we receive from others is what drives our sense of self-worth, we're trying to build on quicksand. All of these things are fickle and subject to change; and if we build our worth on those, then our worth is fickle as well.

Psalm 8 has some better advice for us when we feel worthless.

SEE YOUR SMALLNESS

It might seem strange to start by telling a reader who feels worthless that the way to combat it is to see your smallness, but that's exactly what I'm saying—because that is what David is saying in Psalm 8. To know your worth, you have to first see how small you are. You need to see who you are in the grand scheme of things. So many of our feelings of worthlessness are owing to unrealistic expectations: even God-like expectations. We come up against our inability to get our to-do list done, or to meet all our family's needs or even our own needs, and we feel worthless. We feel small. We feel weak.

And we are small and weak, because we are not God.

Psalm 8 directs our gaze to our majestic God. The theme of the psalm is found in the first and last verses, which use a literary device called an "inclusio." The repeated statement bookends the psalm and tells us what it is about:

> O LORD, our Lord,
>   how majestic is your name in all the earth! (v 1)

> O LORD, our Lord,
>   how majestic is your name in all the earth! (v 9)

God is the central focus of Psalm 8 and of everything we experience. Psalm 8 tells us to look at this majestic God, who fills the earth with his glory. The first way in which you see your smallness is when you look up at the world that he has made and see that it does not revolve around you. It revolves around someone much grander than you—the Creator. The world, even your loved ones, does not need you to be perfect. We have a perfect Creator. We are liberated by our smallness even as we are humbled by our smallness.

All creation comes from God's hands—the stars, the moon, the heavens, the earth; it's all his (v 3). We see our smallness in the vastness of his creative power. We create on such a small scale compared to the majestic Lord God. I write a book. He spoke this earth into being. I fold the laundry. He put every leaf on every tree. I paint a room. He invented color. It should make us marvel and should humble us as well. We are small; he is not.

But we also see our smallness in how God defeats his enemies:

Out of the mouth of babies and infants,
you have established strength because of your foes,
to still the enemy and the avenger. (v 2)

He silences his enemies through the weakest among us. Babies and infants cannot defeat anyone. We know this. But David is showing us here that God's ways are not our ways. When God works on behalf of his people he does it in such a way that only he gets the glory. There will be no questioning who is mighty to save when God delivers us from evil. So he uses helpless, weak people to do it—like babies and infants.

All throughout Scripture, weakness has been the way in which God works in the world. He used barren Sarai, Rebekah, and Rachel to make a mighty nation (Genesis 11 v 30; 25 v 21; 30 v 1). He used stammering Moses to deliver his people from bondage (Exodus 4 v 10-17). He used a foreign, widowed woman to continue the line to King David (Ruth 4 v 14-22). He used a youngest son, a shepherd-boy, to lead his people (1 Samuel 16 v 11-13)—and to write this psalm. Supremely, God came to earth himself as a baby, took on the form of a servant by becoming human, and died a humbling, horrible death to deliver his people from their sins. God uses weakness to display his glory. He is not looking for people who think positive and tell themselves they're great, but for those who are meek and know their need of him.

And once you realize how small you are, you're ready to marvel:

When I look at your heavens, the work of your
fingers,
the moon and the stars, which you have set in place,
what is man that you are mindful of him,
and the son of man that you care for him? (v 3-4)

Seeing how small we are in God's cosmos leads to seeing how loved we are as his created beings. That's where we get our worth. Our worth is not in what we do, create, or even believe. Our worth is in being created and loved by the Creator. When we see the world and our smallness in it, it humbles us, but it also makes us marvel that God would ever stoop so low as to care for us. It puts us in the right mindset by putting God in his rightful place.

SEE YOUR WORTH

Once David has helped us see our place as created beings in God's created world, he then moves to what we do in that world. While our worth is never found in what we accomplish, God has given us a role to play in his creation. And that, too, should make us humble and cause us to marvel at his care for us. It surely led David there:

> *You have made [humanity] a little lower than the*
> *heavenly beings*
> *and crowned him with glory and honor.*
> *You have given him dominion over the works of your*
> *hands;*
> *you have put all things under his feet,*
> *all sheep and oxen,*
> *and also the beasts of the field,*
> *the birds of the heavens, and the fish of the sea,*
> *whatever passes along the paths of the seas. (v 5-8)*

This is creation language, echoing Genesis 1 v 26-27:

> *Then God said, "Let us make man in our image,*
> *after our likeness. And let them have dominion over*
> *the fish of the sea and over the birds of the heavens*
> *and over the livestock and over all the earth and over*
> *every creeping thing that creeps on the earth."*

So God created man in his own image,
in the image of God he created him;
male and female he created them.

David marvels because he knows how majestic God is, and
so he can't believe that God would use him to rule and reign
over his creation. When was the last time you stopped to
think about what it means to be God's image-bearer? You are
created in God's image, which means you are God's picture
to a watching world. Everything you do can tell the world
what God is like, from your job to your home-managing to
your neighborhood relationships. But you don't just tell a
story; you get to partner with God in his story, by working
where God has put you, cultivating the gifts he has given
you, using the resources he provides for you in proportion
with the energy he has afforded you, and subduing the earth
as countless image-bearers have done before you. Your work,
your life, and your service can all point to his glory. The fact
that he uses any of us should make us marvel in the way that
David does, and cry out, "O Lord, our Lord, how majestic
is your name in all the earth."

This transforms the way we view the things that the world
sees as small and not worth much.

Maybe you just mopped the floor (only to have milk
spilled on it immediately), and you struggle to see how this
work is worth much, or how it leads to praise. Or you work
in a mundane job and can't seem to see the point of it at the
end of a long day. Or you teach toddlers in Sunday School
week after week, and it doesn't feel as flashy as leading the
music on Sunday morning. In the world's eyes these things
might seem less important—less valuable—than the more
results-driven work that we see praised so often. But all of
these things can be worship; they can bring glory to God
and are considered worthwhile to God. Whether we are a

CEO or a street-sweeper, God can and does use what we do in his service to bring him glory and to love the world he has made. There is no job too small in God's kingdom. All work is his work. All work brings glory to him.

Want to know your worth? Look at the one whose image you bear. He sees you as his redeemed and loved child. He invites you to work with him, and he sees you and your labors, even if no one else does. He is pleased with your service, and he forgives your failings. This transforms how we work, serve, and live out our calling as his image-bearers.

THREE THINGS TO REMEMBER WHEN YOU FEEL WORTHLESS

Of course, it is easy to say, "Just meditate on God's strength in weakness and how he has created you, and everything will be fine"—but I know that's not always true. Even those with the best theology often find themselves like my friend at the beginning of this chapter—surveying their life and feeling that they are worthless. So, here are some truths to remember when you're in that place.

We feel worthless when we forget that we are all image-bearers with a part to play. Romans 12 v 3-8 is helpful here:

> *For by the grace given to me I say to everyone among you not to think of himself more highly than he ought to think, but to think with sober judgment, each according to the measure of faith that God has assigned. For as in one body we have many members, and the members do not all have the same function, so we, though many, are one body in Christ, and individually members one of another. Having gifts that differ according to the grace given to us, let us use them: if prophecy, in proportion to our faith; if service, in our serving; the one who teaches, in his*

teaching; the one who exhorts, in his exhortation;
the one who contributes, in generosity; the one who
leads, with zeal; the one who does acts of mercy, with
cheerfulness.

You are part of a body (the church), and in the human body every part is necessary for the body to thrive. The same is true for you. You matter. You were created in God's image with specific gifts and abilities that only you can bring to the table. When we forget that, we question our worth.

We feel worthless when we forget that we are image-bearers designed to reflect him and not ourselves. Our work, gifts, service, and very lives should declare his glory. An image doesn't exist for itself. It's meant to (and is able to) point to something greater, and in our case that greater thing is the Creator of the universe—God. We can be who God made us to be in freedom because we know he created us for himself. The world might compare us to everyone else and make us feel small, but the world is a harsh master. God is not, and he is pleased with us when we remember that we work for his glory, not ours.

We feel worthless when we forget that we are all image-bearers, not competitors. How often do we feel worthless because we take our eyes off our own race (Hebrews 12 v 1-2) and instead look at the race of the one next to us? We see a better mom, a better friend, a better wife, a better employee, a better church member, or a better athlete, and we feel insignificant, envious, worthless. But if everyone is an image-bearer, then everyone has a role. You can do what God created you for with joy, not jealousy. This is not a competition.

When we stand back and look at what God has done in the world, in us, and in the universe, we marvel. You might feel worthless, but that doesn't mean you're right. You may be weak, but that doesn't mean God won't use you. He uses the weak and small to shame the strong and let the world see his greatness.

There is not a worthless bone in your body. You matter. You are saved. You are loved. You are useful to God. Worthlessness isn't in your DNA. God's image is.

Extra Psalms: Psalms 24, 33, 76, 139

Journaling

WEARY
PSALMS 42 & 43

Why are you cast down, O my soul,
and why are you in turmoil within me?
Hope in God; for I shall again praise him,
my salvation and my God.

Psalm 43 v 5

"Are we there yet?"

It's a question we hear often on our long car rides to visit family. What begins as an adventurous trip across the country quickly descends into a series of persistent demands to know exactly how much longer we have to go until we get to our destination. The snacks aren't cutting it anymore. The books have lost their interest. Even iPads and movies can't mask the frustration with how long the trip has become.

"How much longer?" they ask.

"Just a few more hours," we say.

"How much longer?" they ask, not even five minutes later.

"What did we just tell you?" we say, frustration mounting.

"HOW MUCH LONGER?" they beg.

Because our children don't have a concept of time yet, an answer that details the hours remaining doesn't help them.

To them, a few minutes feel like a few hours. And in the passage of a few minutes they are still bored, still tired, and still ready to be out of their seats.

To be honest, I don't handle these persistent questions well. There is only so much you can handle when you hear the same question over and over again in a matter of minutes. Add crying (theirs, usually) to the mix, and my plans for our time of family fun move into dreams of a kid-free vacation.

Thankfully, God doesn't handle my persistent questions of "How long?" in the same frustrated tone I use with my kids.

Psalms 42 and 43 are some of the most familiar psalms when it comes to addressing our feelings. Who hasn't cried out with the psalmist, *When is this going to end?* (For "this," think of experiences like your feelings of loneliness, your feelings of despair, your inability to cope with all that life throws at you, your physical pain, your sorrow, your relational conflict… or whatever "this" is causing you to feel weary before you even open your eyes in the morning.) For the psalmist, his "this" is two-fold. He is weary because of his life circumstances. But he's also weary from asking God to intervene and to come close to him, and yet still feeling so far from God and that God is not reaching down to help him. Repeated, continual, and unending trials make even the most devoted Christian weary, especially when we are asking God to intervene.

And it's in that emotional place that Psalms 42 and 43 are written. The general theme of speaking to your soul in distress is carried from Psalm 42 into Psalm 43; and because most people view them as a unit, we'll look at them together. In the original manuscripts they were grouped together. They even use the same phrases in some spots.

WHY SO CAST DOWN?

When you look at these two psalms as one unit, they can be divided into three sections. Each section ends with the same refrain:

Why are you cast down, O my soul,
 and why are you in turmoil within me?
Hope in God; for I shall again praise him,
 my salvation and my God. (42 v 5-6, 11; 43 v 5)

In each section, the psalmist's feelings are on full display, and those feelings lead him to ask these questions.

In 42 v 1-4, he feels despair. He feels far off from God, which is the worst thing he can think of. He is taunted by his enemies, who see and mock his distance from God. He is like a deer panting for water—thirsty for God—yet for some reason he is unable to get to God in worship. The deer is desperate for water, for without it, it will die. The psalmist is desperate for God, for without him, he will die.

He is sad—so sad that crying is all he can do day and night (v 3). His despair only grows as his mind pictures what his life used to be like. Memory heightens despair:

These things I remember,
 as I pour out my soul:
how I would go with the throng
 and lead them in procession to the house of God
with glad shouts and songs of praise,
 a multitude keeping festival. (v 4)

Wisely, in his praying he remembers God's past faithfulness. This is supposed to bring healing, but here when he remembers the past, he sees all the more that his present circumstances are everything but that which he is longing for.

This is why he is so weary. He asks all these questions and doesn't get relief.

His soul resides in the depths (v 6), even though he knows it shouldn't (v 5). And that is only intensified by his understanding that it is God who has placed him in this turmoil:

All your breakers and your waves
have gone over me. (v 7)

Spurgeon said:

"As in a waterspout, the deeps above and below clasp
hands, so it seemed to [him] that heaven and earth
united to create a tempest around him."
(Treasury of David, Volume One, page 274)

I know how he feels.

THE PAIN OF A GOOD MEMORY

After we had been married a little over a year, we were excited to find that I was pregnant. We held on to that secret with expectant joy. Even though we told a few people, it was mostly our private blessing—one we talked about and planned for with hope.

But the hope quickly vanished. I miscarried the baby.

For months, when I looked at our wedding pictures or saw any memory of life before we saw the faint pink lines in our pregnancy-test results, I cried. The memory of life before brought pain. Like the psalmist, when I remembered life before we lost the baby, it only reminded me of a better time, a life in which pain didn't live with us. It reminded me of better days, and I wept. And I felt so, so weary.

Are you weary? Do you share the feelings of the psalmist as you cry out to God day and night? This is why these psalms are here. They remind you that, whatever the particular causes of your struggle, you are not the only one who experiences such weariness. The psalmist gets you. God gets you. And even better than that, God validates your feelings by giving you familiar friends in psalms like these.

HARD QUESTIONS, STRONG PLEAS

If Psalm 42 is about the psalmist dealing with his feelings about his saddened state, Psalm 43 ups the game and begs God to act. The psalmist wrestles with his feelings by asking hard questions and making strong pleas.

- "When shall I come and appear before God?" (42 v 2)
- "Why have you forgotten me?" (42 v 9)
- "Why have you rejected me?" (43 v 2)
- "Send out your light and truth." (43 v 3)

Do you cry out to God day and night, and find that he just isn't showing up? Does your repeated prayer of desperation lead to even more weariness? Like my children, who reach the edge of despair at the end of a long car ride, we have times when we ask the same question again and again, and find that God will not answer in the way we ask him to. It's exhausting to cry out day and night. It's exhausting to cry until there are no tears left. It's exhausting to remember all the things that God has done, only to be reminded of what we don't have now, or of what God seems not to be doing now. It's exhausting to be persistent—and yet the psalmist continues to persist with his pleas and his questions.

You, too, are invited to ask hard questions. Be persistent with your requests to God. Psalm 42 and Psalm 43 teach us that honesty in our questions is important and good. Where else can we go with the angst in our soul but to God? Yet we are tempted towards a lot of different ways of dealing with our angst. Maybe you don't want to run to anyone, including God; instead you prefer to bottle it up, pretending everything is fine. Maybe you want to let it all out, but to do so in a mad rush of rage over your circumstances. Whether you are tempted to give up, bottle up, or rage, the difference between a Christian and non-Christian is not whether we experience these times of wearying burdens but that Christians have a God who is ready and willing to hear from us about them. As Spurgeon wrote:

> "Faith is allowed to enquire of her God the causes
> of his displeasure, and she is even permitted to
> expostulate with him and put him in mind of his
> promises, and ask why apparently they are not
> fulfilled. If the Lord be indeed our refuge, when we
> find no refuge, it is time to be raising the question,
> 'why is this?'"
>
> (Treasury of David, Volume One, page 274)

But as we ask and question—and yes, that is wearying—we need also to remember what we know, even though that, too, can be wearying, as we've seen. We need to remember what was, and therefore what will be, even when right now it seems so far off:

> Hope in God; for I shall again praise him, my
> salvation and my God. (42 v 5, 11; 43 v 5)

It is this that sustains the psalmist when he doesn't understand what is happening. When he remembers his former life and moans, he can look to God and know that God will one day bring him back to worship. His tears may be his food day and night (v 3), but God has not left him in the day or in the night:

> By day the LORD commands his steadfast love,
> and at night his song is with me,
> a prayer to the God of my life. (42 v 8)

What is so comforting about these psalms is not that there is a swift resolution. There isn't. The comfort lies in seeing that by remembering what God is like, in asking hard questions of his soul, and in pleading with God according to his character, the psalmist finds God in the darkness. The same is true for us. It's a long, hard exercise to discover such hope. But it's a worthwhile one.

So, like the persistent widow in Jesus' parable in Luke 18 v 1-8, we should persist in our prayers to the just Judge of all the earth; we "should always pray and not give up" (v 8, NIV). Ask the hard questions. Keep asking. And trust the Lord's character and his timing.

NOT WITHOUT HOPE

And, as we speak to God, we must also speak to ourselves. The psalmist speaks to his own soul in his distress. The constant refrain that he keeps coming back to is "Why are you cast down, O my soul, and why are you in turmoil within me?" (42 v 5, 11; 43 v 5). And it is to his own soul that the psalmist says three times, since it bears repeating again:

Hope in God; for I shall again praise him,
my salvation and my God. (my emphasis)

What sustains the psalmist? Telling himself that he has hope for the future. He might not be praising the Lord now in the company of God's people, but one day he will. He knows his identity is in the Lord, and his salvation and security is sure. He was made to worship, and worship he will.

If you think of the trajectory of the psalms, this makes perfect sense. Psalm 1 tells us of the blessed life and the outcome of the blessed life—you will grow and be sustained by God. Psalm 150, the very last psalm in the Psalter, tells us the final outcome of all of our lives—endless praise. And in the middle we get Psalms 42 and 43, when we don't feel the truth of Psalm 1 and we seem a long way from Psalm 150, and we're weary of life's circumstances and our own confusion:

Hope in God; for [you] shall again praise him.
(42 v 5, 11; 43 v 5)

So, talk to yourself, out loud if it helps. Tell yourself what you know to be true—true of God and, therefore, true of you and of the future. For the Christian, talking to yourself in this way is not a sign of madness; it's a sign of maturity.

And keep talking to God. Ask the questions. Be persistent. Be like the child who asks, "Are we there yet?" every five minutes. Be honest again and again and again. Like our wearied children, we are on a long journey, and we don't know when it will end, but we know that it will someday. In the weariness, there is hope. The burdened weariness will give way to joyful worship. Some trips are longer than others, but every trip has an end. *It will come.* You will again praise God. Unlike the parent who gets bothered by the repeated asking, God can handle all of your questions, even the same ones over and over again.

Come to me all who are weary and burdened, and I
will give you rest. (Matthew 11 v 28, NIV)

Extra Psalms: Psalms 25, 56 (another psalm where the writer talks to himself)

Journaling

HELPLESS
PSALM 46

God is our refuge and strength,
a very present help in trouble.

Psalm 46 v 1

I don't have a lot of psalms committed to memory, but this one is burned into my brain. I have this psalm mostly memorized not because I spent time memorizing it but because I have had to remind myself of its truths over and over again. I can think of several specific times in my life when these words have come to mind, but one time in particular stands out. It is the reason this book is even in existence.

As I mentioned in the Introduction, the psalms became my lifeline when I spent weeks on hospital bed-rest, wondering if I or my son would live. The psalms gave me words for my anguish and my fear. The psalms comforted me in my pain. The psalms reminded me of God and his care and his power.

When I remember Psalm 46, I weep. I think I always will.

A WORD IN THE STORM
This is a psalm of trust. It's a psalm for the one who is utterly and completely helpless in the face of horrifying

uncertainty. The psalmist is contrasting the thing that we think is stable and unmovable (mountains) with the thing that we can know is stable and unmovable (our Creator and Sustainer).

> *Therefore we will not fear though the earth gives way,*
>   *though the mountains be moved into the heart of*
>   *the sea,*
> *though its waters roar and foam,*
>   *though the mountains tremble at its swelling.*
>
> (v 2-3)

Sometimes it feels as if everything around us is crashing down. Sometimes it feels as if what we once thought was unchanging and stable is actually a roaring ocean, and we are being swallowed up by it. The psalmist looks around at his life and he sees only crumbling mountains. Of course, he's exaggerating here (these aren't literal mountains moving), but he's also being honest. And the structure of this psalm follows a pattern of real-life honesty about what is happening to real-life trust in the God who is over it all. The psalmist is using hyperbole to show what he feels—and to urge himself to trust God in the midst of circumstances that have rendered him helpless.

The imagery is vivid. We begin with a declaration of trust—something we are going to need because of what happens right after verse 1: "Therefore we will not fear though the earth gives way." The psalmist is clearly helpless. We don't know the specifics, but he feels so helpless that it's as if the earth is literally shaking on its foundations. There is no stability, and there is nothing he can do to regain his balance.

But God...

God is with his people, even when all around is falling apart. You might feel helpless, but God never is. God is not just there—he is here. He is present. And not just present, but "very present." This is the theme of the psalm: God's constant presence.

- "God is in the midst of [his people; they] shall not be moved" (v 5).
- "The LORD of hosts is with us; the God of Jacob is our fortress" (v 7).
- "Come, behold the works of the LORD" (v 8).
- "Be still, and know that I am God" (v 10).
- "The LORD of hosts is with us; the God of Jacob is our fortress" (v 11).

The earth is raging. The enemies surround us. But God is there. And in that, we have hope. Sometimes a psalm of distress is filled with a long line of cries saying, "How long, O LORD?" and sometimes it is filled with line after line of trust even when the ground beneath is crumbling. This is that psalm. And it's a comfort when you find yourself in frightening circumstances.

FROM RAGING OCEANS TO FLOWING RIVERS

Because the psalms are poetry, the psalmist uses contrast to prove to us God's sustaining care.

> *There is a river whose streams make glad the city of*
> *God,*
> *the holy habitation of the Most High.*
> *God is in the midst of her; she shall not be moved;*
> *God will help her when morning dawns.*
> *The nations rage, the kingdoms totter;*
> *he utters his voice, the earth melts.*
> *The LORD of hosts is with us;*
> *the God of Jacob is our fortress. (v 4-7)*

Notice the contrast. In verses 2-3, it's a raging ocean that threatens the faith of the psalmist. The waters are threatening to swallow up the mountains and the psalmist too. These waters can't be trusted. But God is a refuge for his people, so he has hedged him in. How? With another body of water. In the midst of the raging storm and seas, this image of a river calms the soul and reminds us that God is near and God is sustaining. He has given his servants a peace—peace like a river, you might say.

I'm not one to spend much time in bodies of water (unless you count a pool in the summer), so my experience of them is limited, but even I can find the contrast here helpful. Of course, rivers can swell and rage too. But the psalmist is setting us up to see the character of God by contrasting a peaceful river that nourishes his servant with a vast, raging, unpredictable ocean that swallows his servant whole. There is water that gives life (the river) and water that destroys (the ocean).

This is not the first time that rivers point to God's provision and protection of his people. In Ezekiel 47, the prophet is given a vision for the new Jerusalem, and at its heart is a river: not just any river but a river that gives life (Ezekiel 47 v 7-10, 12). The future reality promised to God's people is one where a body of water doesn't destroy, but instead gives life and peace forever. This theme is taken up again in Revelation 7 v 17 and 21 v 9 – 22 v 5, where John paints the picture of a river that will sustain God's city—his people and his creation—for all eternity. And even more than that, God will be in her midst. The darkness will be gone. The tears will be dried. And worship will be on the city's lips.

But, powerfully, this is not just a future reality. It can be a present experience too. Jesus said:

> *If anyone thirsts, let him come to me and drink.*
> *Whoever believes in me, as the Scripture has said,*
> *"Out of his heart will flow rivers of living water."*
> *(John 7 v 37-38)*

This river of living water is the promised Holy Spirit whom Jesus would send after his death and resurrection (v 39). So the presence of the Lord, who is our refuge and strength, is a present reality for us as well as a future hope. When we read of this river in Psalm 46 and wonder whether and how we might know this kind of peace amid the shaking mountains, John tells us to look no further than God himself. He hasn't left us as orphans. He has come to us and is our refuge in the storm. God dwells in us and with us (John 14 v 18). He cannot be taken from us. Even if everything is shaking, he is not moved.

When you are helpless, there can be a peace. God has secured you. He will nourish you by the power of the Holy Spirit, through the word. He will sustain you by his power. He will care for you by providing the living waters right now. He will be your refuge. And one day, you will drink from these living waters forever.

LOOKING FROM A DIFFERENT ANGLE

The psalms are filled with loud cries of lament to God. Some of them are in this book. And there is a place for complaining to God in our helplessness. Feeling like your world is caving in on you is cause for lament and questioning. It's cause for begging for help from the only One who can deliver you. But there is a sweetness about Psalm 46 that brings perspective and hope.

One of the earliest Bible study questions I learned to ask was "When you see a 'therefore,' ask what the therefore is there for." And we have a "therefore" in Psalm 46:

> *God is our refuge and strength,*
> *a very present help in trouble.*
> ***Therefore*** *we will not fear though the earth gives*
> *way… (v 1-2, my emphasis)*

Because God is our refuge and strength—because he is near and present and strong—we have an antidote to fear. This psalm is one of great helplessness. Everything is falling apart, but the psalmist remembers the character of God, and he is sustained. The "therefore" is the hinge of trust. It is essentially saying, *I will trust the God who is my refuge and so I will not be scared, in spite of the entire earth giving way.*

I said at the beginning that this psalm is one of trust. The psalmist begins by telling us what could lead to fear and helplessness (his world falling apart), and then he moves to the "why" of his trust—his reason for it. In verse 6, he picks up this language of rage and toppling powers, as we see in verse 2, but it's not his security that is falling here. It's those who oppose God who are falling.

> *The nations rage, the kingdoms totter;*
> *he utters his voice, the earth melts.*
> *The Lord of hosts is with us;*
> *the God of Jacob is our fortress. (v 6-7)*

It's almost as if he turns his helpless insecurities on their head and says, *Want to know what is really going to topple? Not my world, but God's enemies. I can lose everything without losing what I truly need, for my God is in the midst of my life.* That is how we find trust when we are helpless. God is never helpless, as we're reminded by the contrast again in this language of toppling, raging, shattering, and fighting (v 6-9). When our mountains are crumbling and the ocean of our life is raging, verses 6-10 turn our gaze towards the God who not only is with us but will deal with every last enemy and helpless circumstance one day. "Come, behold the works of the Lord," he says (v 8). "Be still and know that I am God," he says (v 10). He will win. He will always win. He is here. He will always be here. You might be helpless, but he never will be. The God who has always existed and has been keeping his people throughout the centuries is your fortress (v 11).

Declaring what is true about God's power and care does not remove the difficulties we face. Life is scary. Suffering is real. And we really are helpless. We really are powerless. So often we can't change our circumstances. But the psalmist isn't brushing aside the reality of this world. He is simply reminding himself of the One who is stronger than anything he faces or any loss he experiences. The seas may rage, but he knows the One who controls the wind and the seas (Mark 4 v 35-41). The mountains may topple, but he knows the One who created the mountains (Genesis 1 v 1; Psalm 24 v 1).

While our helplessness often leads us to lament (and that is a good and right response), our helplessness need never cause us to despair or give up. But God… Feeling helpless is the ground for growing our trust and enjoying God's power. Psalm 46 teaches us that.

God is "a very present help" in trouble. He is a helper who is always there when there is trouble. It doesn't remove the trouble. It doesn't remove the helplessness. It doesn't remove the scary things that lie before you. But it does anchor you. He is your refuge and strength. He is with you. He is your peace.

This journal entry from my time on bed-rest captures my feelings on Psalm 46 well:

> *"As Jeff [one of our pastors] shared yesterday, God's not far off. Not only is he a fortress but he's very near. Very present. The psalm goes on to use his nearness as the assurance of our hope in trials. It doesn't remove the difficulty. It anchors us to his presence that never leaves. 'God is in the midst of her. She shall not be moved. God will help her when morning dawns' (Psalm 46 v 5). Sometimes the*

thought of a new day feels terrifying. Morning looms large and heavy and uncertain. Morning also feels like an eternity away when I can't sleep. Morning means more unknown. More fears. But if God is a very present help in trouble, then I don't need to fear the morning. His presence and help will be as near as it was the day before."

One of our pastors had texted lines from Psalm 46 to me the day before, so I spent much of the next day reading it and meditating on it. It didn't change the fact that I was stuck in a hospital bed. It didn't change the fact that my son (or I) could die within a matter of minutes. It didn't change the fact that my other three children were scared and suffering upheaval because both parents were gone for an extended period of time. It didn't change my circumstances. But it did lift my gaze. Some psalms express your feelings for you. Some psalms make you feel something you weren't feeling before you read them. This one made me feel trust and hope, even when helplessness was crushing me.

When the mountains around you threaten to topple into the raging storm of your life, I pray you will remember the "therefore." You might be unable to find stable footing in your trial, but God is always stable. He is always immovable. He is your refuge. You can trust him and sing with the psalmist, "We will not fear." You may be helpless, but you need never be hopeless.

Extra Psalms: Psalms 28, 54, 79, 124

Journaling

GRIEF
PSALM 31

Be gracious to me, O Lᴏʀᴅ, for I am in distress;
my eye is wasted from grief;
my soul and my body also.

Psalm 31 v 9

G rief is a harsh master. It is a whole-body experience. It affects everything in you, from the inside out. It steals your strength. It laughs at your sighing. It crushes you. It leaves you alone for a while, before returning suddenly as a sudden phrase, a picture, a smell, or even a person brings it all back, and you are undone.

David knew this. We know this.

I have a note in my Bible marked 4/1/11 right next to this verse. If you look closely, you will see tearstains scattered around it. Nine months before that day I had seen those two hoped-for pink lines: I was pregnant.

And then I wasn't.

As quickly as the lines appeared, the hoped-for baby vanished, leaving me to question over and over again if I had ever truly been pregnant. But the grief that lingered reminded me every single day that my body had once held a baby, though my arms would not. There I was, alone in our apartment, not pregnant and, it appeared, unable to get pregnant again.

The due date was April 2, but I wanted that day to just pass by without fanfare. I thought that if I pretended it wasn't on the calendar then maybe it wouldn't hurt as bad. I now know that that is impossible. So it was on the eve of the day when our child should have been born that I sat down to read the psalms. I marked the date beside these verses, because Psalm 31 was my prayer to God. I remember how my grief rushed up on me. In the days leading up to the due date, I had felt very little. And then, with the pages of the Bible open in front of me, the grief poured out. David is speaking of a personal crisis in this psalm, so he uses the personal pronouns "I," "me," and "my," and they helped me pray back to God everything I felt. I wanted the Lord to turn his ear toward me in my sorrow (v 2). I wanted to believe that he had seen my affliction and distress (v 7). I suddenly felt wasted away with grief, and I needed him to be gracious to me (v 9). I recounted my year of sorrow to the only One who could truly hear and understand and heal.

While David uses the word "grief" in the psalm (v 9), it's not clear that he means bereavement. A variety of things were going on that could have caused David's grief (enemies, physical suffering, or a hyper-awareness of sin that leads to grief). But the psalm is broad enough to carry the weight of whatever grief you are experiencing—including bereavement but not limited to it.

The dictionary defines grief as "a deep sorrow, especially that caused by someone's death." We tend to reserve the word for our response to the loss of life. But, as Cameron Cole, who suffered the grief of the death of his young son, points out, grief is a weight that is borne by all those who have suffered the loss of something dear to them:

*"All grief involves loss. A joyful hope for the future
dies, or a cherished aspect of the present slips into the
past. And we grieve."* *(thegospelcoalition.org/article/
misunderstood-grief, accessed 3/22/19)*

Almost all of us are carrying grief, whether its cause was just
last week or many years ago. You feel grief in the death of a
marriage, the death of a career, or the death of a friendship,
as well as in the death of a loved one. Your hope for life is
dashed in the death of a dream or expectations for the future.
And if you haven't experienced grief, live long enough and
you will. It's a horrible, inevitable result of living in a broken
world. There are some of you walking through a grief that
is much more painful than my own—a grief that seems too
much to bear, a grief that makes you feel that nothing can
ease your pain. I hope Psalm 31 can speak into your grief.

THE BACK-AND-FORTH OF REAL LIFE

Like a lot of the psalms, this one goes back and forth. It
begins with trust, then moves to cries, then moves to trust,
then moves to cries, and then ends with a corporate plea
for trust. The back-and-forth nature of this psalm makes it
harder to outline—but it makes it completely relatable to
our experience of walking through grief.

Suffering and grief are not linear. Counselors talk about
five stages of grief, but they often tell people that you can
move between the stages much more fluidly than you would
expect. In other words, you can go from acceptance back to
depression in an instant, and sometimes stay there for a long
time. (See, for example, https://grief.com/the-five-stages-of-
grief/, accessed January 24, 2019.)

David is experiencing that here.

While the middle of the psalm (v 9) contains this refer-
ence to his eyes being wasted with grief, much of the psalm

is filled with a back-and-forth monologue in which he begs God for relief and trust. The beginning verses alternate between pleas and trust (v 1-8), but then the middle verses give us the reasons for the back-and-forth (v 9-13). David tells us of his grief, and then it explains it in further detail. Then he goes back to the pleas for help and trust (v 14-24), with trust being the predominant theme at the end.

HONEST PLEAS ABOUT A HARD SITUATION

David is utterly honest. He has begged God for relief and protection. He has begged God to lead and guide him. He has begged God to sustain him. He has begged God to be gracious to him. He has begged God to listen to him. And then he tells us why. It's almost as if he gets to verses 9-10 and just can't contain his emotions any longer.

> *Be gracious to me, O LORD, for I am in distress;*
> *my eye is wasted from grief;*
> *my soul and my body also.*
> *For my life is spent with sorrow,*
> *and my years with sighing;*
> *my strength fails because of my iniquity,*
> *and my bones waste away.*

It's just too much. Even with all of the reminders of God's strong hand of protection and deliverance, the weight of his sorrow is crushing him. His life and years have been spent with "sighing," or "groaning," as the Christian Standard Bible puts it. He's utterly exhausted by his crying. Do you have a years-long grief weighing heavy on you—or are you looking at the prospect of those years stretching ahead? Here, in Psalm 31, you find a familiar friend: tears, sighing, groaning, and crying are part of what it means to be a human in a world that regularly breaks us. Being honest with God is part of what it means to grieve well. Just listen to what one pastor says about the importance of honest emotions in our grief:

> *"You can pray in faith and dissolve into a flood of tears. David knows God has delivered him and will deliver him, yet his eyes still weep and waste away. One of the worst things you can say to a Christian brother or sister is not to cry when he or she is going through something really hard. 'Have faith,' someone will say, 'don't get emotional.' David trusted God, and his eyes still 'wasted from grief.' Our Lord Jesus trusted his Father, but he wept at Lazarus's tomb even though he knew he would raise Lazarus from the tomb just minutes later. We can believe with all our heart that God will raise our loved one from the grave and still cry because [they are] gone."*
> *(James Johnston, The Psalms: Rejoice the Lord is King, Volume 1, pages 321-322)*

But these middle verses give us more explanation of why David is facing such grief. His honesty continues. In verse 11 he says he has become a reproach to (or been ridiculed by) his adversaries, and in verse 13 he faces gossip and whispers from all sides. But in verse 12 we see the saddest cause of his grief:

> I have been forgotten like one who is dead;
> I have become like a broken vessel.

As I said, grief is a tricky business. The grieving person needs most to be remembered and pursued by friends who care and aren't afraid of the grief—and here, what is hurting David is that he is experiencing the reverse. He is being mocked, gossiped about, and forgotten by all around him. The grief and suffering make those who see him doubt God and his care. They make his enemies more critical. They make his friends more distant. Grief can do that to our friends. They don't know what to say, so they say nothing. They don't know what questions to ask, so they talk about benign things that have nothing to do with your sorrow. But it only makes you feel more isolated. More alone. More forgotten. David understands those feelings well, and if David understands them, then God does so even more because he inspired David to pen these words.

TRUST WHEN YOU'RE BREAKING

When we are weighed down by grief, we often find trust and grief living in the same train of thought, much like David did. We vacillate between the plea "Be a rock of refuge for me, a strong fortress to save me!" (v 2) and the declaration "For you are my rock and my fortress" (v 3).

In the plea, you get the trust. In asking God to be something for you, you find out that he already is what you are begging him to be.

The height of trust in this psalm comes after the middle section of deep anguish (v 9-13). David is in distress. David is grieved. And where does he go? What does he say?

> *But I trust in you, O LORD:*
> *I say, "You are my God."*
> *My times are in your hand;*
> *rescue me from the hand of my enemies and from*
> *my persecutors! (v 14-15)*

"But" is the word that all trust hinges on. In effect, David is saying, *Yes, it's bad. Yes, I'm grieving. Yes, I'm forgotten. But…* There is another layer to the reality he's experiencing: God is at work.

There is so much to grieve, and so much to break me, but I trust in God, David says. That is faith. It's a faith that comes after much honesty and much wrestling with God. It's faith that comes in the midst of your world being shaken. That's a genuine, tested faith (1 Peter 1 v 6-7).

And it is a faith in God's sovereign goodness: "My times are in your hand" (Psalm 31 v 15). This is the basis for David's trust and ours as well. God is sovereign. Our times are his. This is the doctrine of God's providence. Charles Spurgeon says, "Providence is a soft pillow for anxious heads" (*The Treasury of David,* page 62). The pastor Alistair Begg says that this verse is...

> "... how we can even get up in the morning. It's an expression of trust even when we don't know how it will turn out."
>
> (My Times Are in His Hands, sermon)

Saying "my times are in his hand" does not remove our grief, and it doesn't change our circumstances. But it does comfort us in the crushing sadness of grief.

In many ways, this acknowledgment is what leads to a shift in the psalm's tone. David's pleas turn from grief-stricken to hopeful. His cries are less frequent, and his trust begins to take center stage. While we see trust begin to grow and flourish in the remainder of the psalm, we should not see this psalm as a simple formula for getting the grieving person to turn from grief to trust. Instead, we should see it as the fruit of working through grief rightly. You cry out to God in honesty. You ask him to do for you what he says in his word he will do. You appeal to his character. And then you wait for trust to grow.

That might take years. After all, the psalms are poems. Some poems are written in a moment, some over a lifetime. I once heard a Psalms scholar, Mark Futato, say on a podcast something to the effect of, "The psalmists may have started one in November and ended it in August."

Sometimes in the throes of grief you don't feel trust. But you can get there eventually. David encourages us to get there eventually. You don't have to wait for grief to fade before you trust, because sometimes it never fades. But you can find yourself experiencing this surprising paradox of joy and grief, trust and sorrow.

TRUST AS YOU WAIT

This is where David gets to in this psalm. In fact, the last few verses of this psalm contain more trust than plea. And as the trust grows, the audience for the trust expands. Many of the psalms end with a corporate element like this.

> *Love the LORD, all you his saints!*
> *The LORD preserves the faithful*
> *but abundantly repays the one who acts in pride.*
> *Be strong, and let your heart take courage,*
> *all you who wait for the LORD! (v 23-24)*

David wants you to learn from him. We are never alone in our suffering or in our deliverance. And when God acts in our lives, we should tell his people about it. When we suffer, we suffer as a body. When we are delivered, we are delivered for the body of Christ. As Paul tells us in Romans 12 v 15, the Christian life is one of community where we "rejoice with those who rejoice [and] weep with those who weep." *See how God has worked in my life,* David says, *and trust him. He is worth it.*

The journey to trust in the face of grief is often hard and long. But if our times are truly in his hands, then trust will come. As you wait, cling on and gaze up, my friends. He will not leave you. Morning is coming.

Extra Psalms: Psalms 80, 126, 137

Journaling

ENVY
PSALM 73

Truly God is good to Israel,
to those who are pure in heart.
But as for me, my feet had almost stumbled,
my steps had nearly slipped.
For I was envious of the arrogant
when I saw the prosperity of the wicked.

Psalm 73 v 1-3

Social media is a place for sharing. It's where we share the highs of life—the baby's first steps, our engagement announcement, our new job, even our new home. It's not an uncommon occurrence to see the good news of someone's life. In fact, I usually rejoice with them. It's one of the reasons I love social media. I love seeing the lives of people I knew growing up, or from college, or even from my own church.

But this particular time, I didn't love it. I was mindlessly scrolling through social media when I happened upon a post from someone who was clearly prospering in work. And I knew something about this particular person. I knew that they were sneaky and dishonest, and used people to get ahead. So when I looked at their success, all I could think was, "This is not fair." It wasn't just that I didn't like what they had; seeing their success made me painfully aware of things we lacked. I knew dishonesty was the way they had got ahead, and I knew that we had been honest in ways they hadn't. We deserved better, I thought.

And I didn't stop there.

I stewed. I thought about all the ways in which our family was better. I judged this person. I judged all those congratulating the person.

And I was envious.

What do you do when the wicked prosper? Do you do what I did—stew in envy and anger? Do you cry out, maybe only under your breath, "This is not fair"? It's hard when you see someone who mocks God and yet is getting married, while you struggle with your singleness. Or you see someone living in willful rebellion against her Creator and building her dream house, while you worry about the leaking roof and mold. Or maybe you are being bullied and mistreated by someone whom everyone seems to love and wants to be around, while you can't name a single close friend. What do you do when the wicked prosper?

Within days of my social-media-prompted bout of envy, I happened to land on Psalm 73, and I found a friend—for its writer, Asaph, was also threatened by envy of the wicked.

You've likely heard verses from Psalm 73 before. Does this look familiar?

Whom have I in heaven but you? And there is nothing on earth that I desire besides you. My flesh and my heart may fail, but God is the strength of my heart and my portion forever.

It's Psalm 73 v 25-26. These are popular verses, aren't they? But these verses of great worship come near the end of a psalm of great anguish, a psalm of great questioning, a psalm where Asaph's faith is on the edge. These verses are the pinnacle of Psalm 73—it's the great resolution after a period of great struggle. We need to see the struggle first, before we can get to the worship.

But first, who was Asaph? He was a descendant of Levi and one of the temple musicians (1 Chronicles 6 v 39; 16 v 15). He was regarded as one of the godly: the men who brought praise before the Lord and his people regularly. So it is helpful to us as we enter this psalm, where there is dissonance between what he knows and what he feels, to know that even this godly worship leader had to work through feelings that are common to us all.

THEY'RE DOING WELL

Asaph is clearly struggling with the prosperity that comes to the wicked. He sees a lot of things when he looks at their lives:

- They are well fed and they have no pain (Psalm 73 v 4).
- Their lives aren't as hard as the lives of others.
- They are prideful and violent, but they suffer no adverse consequences.
- They are flagrant in their sin (v 6-7).
- They speak against God, they lie, they mock God, and they doubt that he has any power over their choices (v 9-11).
- Their riches continue to increase (v 12).
- They use and abuse people with no regard for God and no regard for anything other than themselves, and they boast in it.

The wicked have it made, it seems. And don't we see this all around us? Sometimes it appears that Christians have it harder than non-Christians. The ones who openly mock God can have more money and fewer problems than the faithful believers. And yet aren't we meant to know that "God is good to Israel" (v 1), to his people? Like the psalmist, we see the gap between what the Bible declares and what life suggests, and we struggle with our feelings about it. The Bible is full of righteous people who suffer while the wicked prosper. So is life around us.

SEEING PROMPTS FEELING

All of this seeing leads Asaph to feeling: and what he feels is envy (v 3). He feels that his efforts to remain righteous and pure are in vain (v 13). He feels indignation (v 4-10). He feels anger. He feels despair (v 14-16). This is the real struggle of a real person. We are not emotionally neutral about injustice. As image-bearers of God, this is not surprising, because God isn't emotionally neutral either, as we will see later in the psalm.

Verses 12-14 are the height of Asaph's despair:

> *Behold, these are the wicked;*
> *always at ease, they increase in riches.*
> *All in vain have I kept my heart clean*
> *and washed my hands in innocence.*
> *For all the day long I have been stricken*
> *and rebuked every morning.*

He is essentially saying, *Look at how hard I am trying to follow God, while the wicked don't even bother but are still doing better than me. Why even try living as God asks?* "Truly God is good … to those who are pure in heart" (v 1)? Here, having been confronted with the prosperity of the wicked, he essentially throws up his hands. Living for God feels like a futile effort. The wicked are not stricken or rebuked—and yet they deserve to be. Asaph is stricken and rebuked every morning—and yet he doesn't deserve it.

Then he reaches the moment of greatest danger. He allows the prosperity of the wicked to determine what he believes about God and what he thinks about following God. His growing bitterness means that even when he is convicted over his response, he can't truly see his mistake, because his focus is all present and all immediate—he is like a beast (v 21-22).

That's what envy does to him. It makes him like a beast towards God. It makes him angry, wild, and out of control. The truth is that the psalmist's deepest problem is not the injustice he sees, but the envy he feels. And this envy is causing him to believe that this is all there is, that God is not going to win in the end, and that there is no point in following him wholeheartedly. His steps of faith have nearly slipped (v 2).

And haven't we all been there?

Desire for justice is not wrong. In fact it is God-like. God is a God of justice and even demands it. Desire for good things in this life is not wrong. But over-desire for good things—idolatry of them—is. So while we should be angry at injustice, we can never excuse responding in envy to God's choice not to give us certain good things. When we give in to envy, we start to slip. Our faith is at stake. So we need Psalm 73 to teach us how to fight the feeling of envy: how to defeat it and leave it behind, coming out trusting and enjoying God on the other side.

A DIFFERENT WAY OF SEEING THINGS

What gets Asaph from verse 13 ("In vain have I kept my heart clean") to verse 25 ("there is nothing on earth that I desire besides you")? Verses 16-17 are the turning point of the psalm:

> But when I thought how to understand this,
>   it seemed to me a wearisome task,
> until I went into the sanctuary of God;
>   then I discerned their end.

Making sense of it all is a wearisome task until when? Until he goes into the sanctuary of God. It is only there, in God's presence, that he is able to see himself rightly and the wicked rightly:

> *Truly you set them in slippery places;*
>   *you make them fall to ruin.*
> *How they are destroyed in a moment,*
>   *swept away utterly by terrors!*
> *Like a dream when one awakes,*
>   *O LORD, when you rouse yourself, you despise them*
>   *as phantoms. (v 18-20)*

There is no answer to the problem of the prosperity of the wicked apart from looking to God. It is only when Asaph goes to God that he gains perspective on his circumstances. It is only when he looks away from what his eyes can see and looks from God's perspective that he sees clearly. The prosperity that the wicked enjoy now is temporary. In an instant they will be wiped out. Their worldly dreams may have come true, but they're still just dreams—and dreams end.

Here is God's perspective: the wicked will become nothing, and the godly will enjoy the presence of God now and the glory of God forever. In God's presence Asaph gets mercy, despite his previously envious response towards the wicked:

> *I am continually with you;*
>   *you hold my right hand,*
> *You guide me with your counsel,*
>   *and afterward you will receive me to glory.*
>
>   *(v 23-24)*

There is nothing to envy a wicked person for, is there? Think about it: in 200 years, where will the wicked be? They will be in judgment. But for all eternity we get God. There is nothing that we lack or will ever lack, because of what we have been given by God through Christ. On earth, we get God's presence, his counsel, his strength, his love—and then, at the end of our life on this earth, we get a joyful reception from him in glory. That is what the psalmist needed to see. He needed to step back and get God's perspective. He needed to see that while the wicked were prospering in the here and now, it was so very temporary. What is 70 years of ease in comparison to an eternity in judgment? What is 70 years of hardship on this earth in comparison to God's presence guiding us through it and an eternity of glory to come?

This is what Asaph comes to realize as he stands in the sanctuary of God. The psalm ends with praise born out of this new perspective.

For behold, those who are far from you shall perish;
you put an end to everyone who is unfaithful to you.
But for me it is good to be near God;
I have made the LORD *God my refuge,*
that I may tell of all your works. (v 27-28)

The nearness of the Lord is always for our good. The farther away we are from him, the easier it is to forget that he is on the throne, that he has eternal purposes that cannot be thwarted, and that we are his beloved children. Sometimes it takes great wrestling, like it did for Asaph, to get us to the place of seeing him as our good portion, but it's always to our benefit when we do. Asaph couldn't gain any right perspective on his circumstances until he went into the sanctuary—until he looked upward instead of outward.

It is the same for me. The answer to anxiety over my circumstances and envy over others' comfort is never found on social media, in comfort food, in binging on Netflix, or in venting to my friend or husband. Stewing over my envy and anger—though I so often go there first—never helps. The answer to my envy is always to look to the God who is Lord over my circumstances, who is guiding me in my circumstances, and who will take me to glory beyond the ups and downs of this life.

This psalm starts with God and ends with God. It starts in verse 1 almost as if Asaph is telling us what his head knows but his heart just can't get behind: "Truly God is good to Israel, to those who are pure in heart." And then throughout the whole psalm there is a struggle—a struggle for Asaph to remain pure in heart in the face of all that is around him. And in verse 28, we end with the same God that we started with. The God who promised to be good to Israel is the same God who is our portion forever. He is the same God whose nearness is our good. Asaph is saved by God, sustained by God, and kept by God—and so are we. That's what gives him a foothold when he had been slipping—and that's what gives us a firm footing too. It's what gives Asaph contentment when he had previously been consumed with envy. It's what moves us to contentment too.

Without God's perspective, we will only trust what our eyes can see—and what our eyes can see is only a whole lot to be envious of. But when we get near God, we are able to see and feel rightly. We realize that he is all we need and that he is what we most desire. Even when we are scrolling through social media, we are able to say, and enjoy saying:

> *Whom have I in heaven but you, and there is nothing on earth I desire besides you. My flesh and my heart may fail, but God is the strength of my heart and my portion forever. (v 25-26)*

Amen.

Extra Psalms: Psalms 37, 92

Journaling

ASHAMED
PSALM 51

Have mercy on me, O God,
according to your steadfast love;
according to your abundant mercy.

Psalm 51 v 1

There is a category of sin that we are comfortable with in our churches. We may call it sin, but we aren't afraid to talk about it. We casually share it as a prayer request. We may even joke about it. We know others who struggle similarly, and that seems somewhat to excuse it.

But then there are other sins: the ones you don't speak of; the ones that would make your friends distance themselves from you if they knew; the ones that would make even your enemies shudder. These are the sins we don't share in prayer times even with our most trusted, wise sisters, although we really should because we need the help—we need the means of grace and we need forgiveness. But we are scared to talk about them. They're just so awful.

Sin, with all of its promises of fulfillment in the beginning, crushes you in its aftermath.

You are ashamed.

This is how David felt when he penned Psalm 51.

You are likely familiar with the events surrounding David's sin with Bathsheba. In 1 Samuel 11, David sees Bathsheba bathing on her roof, lusts after her, takes her, uses her for sex, and then sends her home. But the story doesn't end there. She gets pregnant, but instead of seeing this as his chance to confess and (as far as possible) make things right, David has her husband killed and takes Bathsheba as his own wife.

The cover-up is complete—except that God does not allow him to get away with it. He sends Nathan the prophet to confront him in chapter 12. David is at last gripped by the reality and gravity of his sin. Confronted with the truth about his murderous, lustful, covetous, and lying plot to have Bathsheba for himself and destroy her husband in the process, David confesses and is broken to his core.

So what does he do? He writes this psalm. He writes a prayer which models for us the right way to come before God with our shame and guilt.

THIS IS YOUR SONG

You can't separate Psalm 51 from David's sin, but its universal nature helps us apply it more broadly. In the heading of the psalm, the very first line is "To the choirmaster," indicating that it was meant to be sung. Charles Spurgeon says:

> *[This is not] written for private meditation only, but for the public service of song. Suitable for the loneliness of individual penitence, this matchless psalm is equally well adapted for an assembly of the poor in spirit. (The Treasury of David, page 401)*

Don't let the heinous nature of David's sin (stealing a man's wife, using her for sex, murdering her husband, trying to cover it up) deter you from seeing Psalm 51 as a psalm for you as well. You may not have done all or any of these things, but David wants us to understand something deeper here.

Sin is serious.

Whether in our current culture a sin is considered big or small, sin is always an offense against God—and so every sin is serious, because God is infinitely holy. There is no sin that is comfortable, excusable, or humorous. There is no sin that is small enough to be brushed off as owing to "tiredness," "human nature," or even "not that big of a deal." Sin is sin, and we must see it the way David (and God) sees it. All of us should feel the shame of our sin. All of us need David to teach us what it looks like to confess, be cleansed, and be restored. Do you sing about your sin and your Savior? According to David, you should.

This psalm is divided into two sections:

1. Repentance and a plea for pardon (v 1-12)
2. Renewal and restored relationship (v 13-19)

In the first half of the psalm, we see what it looks like to be truly broken over our sin, to confess our sin rightly, and to make an appeal to God. In the second half of the psalm, we see what happens both personally and corporately after a sinner is restored to right relationship with God. We acknowledge—we feel—our shame, and we are pardoned. The answer to our guilt is not to deny it but to know what to do with it.

LEARNING TO CONFESS

Feeling ashamed is a normal response when we feel convicted about our sin. It's a sign that the Spirit is at work in us. So what do you do when you feel guilty? Guilt is a powerful force that can either drive us away from God or to God. In Psalm 51, David has stopped running from God and he is running to God. First he appeals to God's mercy, which is his only hope as a broken and needy sinner. We need to see the framework for David's confession (its basis and results) before we look at the confession itself, so we will skip around a bit in the psalm before we get there. Just hang with me!

Have mercy on me, O God,
 according to your steadfast love;
 according to your abundant mercy. (v 1)

We can ask for forgiveness because of who God is and what he has promised. That is why David speaks first of God's mercy and only then of his sin in verse 2. God is holy: that is certain. But the basis for David's appeal here is first the relationship that God has with him. God loves him. God is in covenant relationship with him, as he has been with Israel since he rescued them from Egypt. God is faithful to his covenant people. This theme continues all through the psalm.

Then, in verses 7 and 9, David asks God for cleansing because not only is God merciful, but he is also the only one who can make him clean. This is what leads David to confess his sin. He knows who God is and what God can do. The appeal to God's mercy leads to the appeal to be cleansed by this merciful God, which leads to a restored relationship in verses 10-12. This is the end goal of true repentance. We make an appeal to God based on his character (he is merciful, gracious, and loving towards his children); we ask him to do what only he can do (cleanse us from the inside out); and then we ask him for a restored relationship (because sin has broken our fellowship with him). Repentance is never just for repentance's sake. We always repent with the intention of having a restored relationship.

David has a clear view of his God—and he has a clear view of his sin too:

Against you, you only, have I sinned
 and done what is evil in your sight,
 so that you may be justified in your words
 and blameless in your judgment.
 Behold, I was brought forth in iniquity,
 and in sin did my mother conceive me. (v 4-5)

David isn't saying that his sins against Bathsheba and Uriah are irrelevant. He's using hyperbole to acknowledge that his greatest sin is his offense against God—the sin of rebelling against God's rule that lay behind all those horrendous sins against others. It is not that what he has done to Bathsheba and Uriah is not horrendous—it is that what David has done before God is even worse. We will find no freedom if we don't see our sin first as a sin against God and then as a sin against the ones who bear his image.

So often when we sin against someone, we are broken by the effect it has on the relationship, or the way they view us now, or the way it messes up our life. That breaks us, and it should—but it shouldn't be what breaks us most. What should grip us is the gravity of our sin against a holy God. He is the one we have sinned against, first and foremost.

When we view our sin only in terms of the people we have sinned against, we have no assurance that at some point, things will be ok again. People are horrible masters. Mercy is never a total given with people because, like us, they are sinful. They don't always forgive freely or let our sin go. Even the most forgiving person cannot necessarily erase the relational consequences of our sin. But with God, his mercy is always abundant because of what Christ has done. Guilt before others is crushing. Guilt before God gives hope.

David knows who is his God is. He knows what he is guilty of, and he begs God to cleanse him. In confession, all we bring is a broken heart and empty hands before a holy and merciful God (v 16-17). God does it all. We just receive. We empty our hands of deal-making based on any good behavior (David knows he has none of that here), and then we are able to receive restored relationship from God.

God is gracious as well as holy, merciful as well as just. Yes, David has sinned against God. But he knows God's character, so he appeals to him based on that. This relationship relies on who God is, not on who David is—which, given that David is a miserable sinner, is good news.

WE ARE NOT ALONE

It may look to us as if Psalm 51 could end with verse 12. David has acknowledged and repented of his sin, and cried out for pardon and restoration. But there is more to say, because David's repentance is for the greater good. Having been forgiven, he tells everyone about his salvation: "O LORD, open my lips, and my mouth will declare your praise" (v 15).

Praise is the point of his restoration. God has delivered him from his sin and restored him to right standing with himself. And then, after he speaks of the nature of right sacrifice before God (a humble, broken heart), David speaks of God being ready to receive his physical sacrifices (v 19). David first needed to acknowledge his shame before God, and only then would God remove his shame, restore him, and receive his worship of praise.

But notice that David switches from personal to corporate expression in verse 18:

> *Do good to Zion in your good pleasure;*
> *build up the walls of Jerusalem;*

He has hinted at this wider perspective in verse 13, where he said, "Then I will teach transgressors your ways, and sinners will return to you," but here he speaks specifically of Zion, the place where God's people dwell. Why take such a personal psalm—and shameful sin—and make it about others? Because sin is never just about us individually. It always has a ripple effect. So does our deliverance. God is seen to be holy in our repentance, but he is also seen to be holy in our restoration. This is why it is good to be open (within reason) about our shame and about our salvation. Often in church, we are all busy pretending that we are doing fine, or that our sin isn't that bad. We put on a good front, speaking only generally but not specifically or personally about sin. An outsider might think that the salvation we love to talk about is slightly unnecessary, since we apparently have little to actually be saved from.

David doesn't do that here. He is public about his failure and public about his forgiveness. And when we are like that, it points other sinners towards how they too can be restored. Deep down we know we are as sinful as David, even if we are scared to admit it. When we bring our sin and shame out into the light, it can be dealt with and we can receive the full forgiveness that only God can provide. Verse 18 is making the point to all of us that God builds up his people as his people deeply appreciate his mercy, and we only know that mercy by being open and honest with him and with his people about the sin that makes us need that mercy. When I bury my shame and keep secret my sin, I am actually thinking of my own reputation. When I acknowledge it, and declare the undeserved and wondrous truth that God would save a wretch like me, I am thinking of God's reputation.

So, what are the "small" sins that you find easy to excuse or to justify? Do you need to feel more guilty, more ashamed, about these things, so that you're compelled to cry out for the forgiveness you need for them? Society, and even church, may belittle those sins—God does not.

Alternatively (or perhaps simultaneously), are you burdened by a sin so crushing that you feel you can never share it and don't dare to really believe you're forgiven for it? Take your guilt to God. He pardons abundantly and completely. Guilt and shame can be replaced by gratitude and joy. Sin is serious—and you know that. But God is merciful—and you can know that too.

Extra Psalms: Psalms 39, 130

Journaling

ANXIOUS
PSALM 13

How long will I store up anxious concerns
within me,
agony in my mind every day?

Psalm 13 v 2 (CSB)

If you were to ask a room filled with women what they struggle with most, I think many would say "anxiety." From the woman who has experienced anxiety since the earliest moments of her life to the woman who first met anxiety as she was tossed about by the ever-shifting friendship groups of little girls, or crammed for a test in college, or started to navigate a workplace or the uncertainties of parenting, anxiety plagues so many of us in a number of ways.

Anxiety certainly plagues me. Perhaps—whether constantly or periodically—it does you, too.

Often when we talk about anxiety, we think about it in terms of a spiral. You lose a job, or you remember a previous trauma, or you have a really stressful week, or your friend betrays you; and the next thing you know, your thoughts are gripped by "what-ifs" and "I can'ts" and "how cans," and you are flooded with anxiety. You can't find equilibrium. You feel you are spiraling out of control.

A friend of mine compares it to a tornado: a giant vortex of unrelenting stress and confusion—a force so powerful that it sucks up everything in its path and then spits you back out as a gnarled, unrecognizable shell of a person. For some of us the feeling slowly builds, like a powerful summer storm; but for others it will rush upon you for no apparent reason and with no real warning. One moment you are brushing your teeth and getting ready for bed—the next moment your chest is tight, your breath is short, and you are in a panic over your circumstances or your perception of them.

Anxiety is a nasty feeling. At times it seems impossible to overcome. That is why Psalm 13 is so fitting for the anxious person. It begins at the outset with a litany of "How long?" questions:

> How long, O LORD? Will you forget me forever?
>   How long will you hide your face from me?
>   How long must I take counsel in my soul
>   and have sorrow in my heart all the day?
>   How long shall my enemy be exalted over me? (v 1-2)

Anxious people are often told that each day carries enough of its own burdens, so being anxious about tomorrow won't help much. That's true (Matthew 6 v 34). There is not a lot we can do about hypotheticals. But what David is describing is not a simple and fairly rational fear about tomorrow. Anxiety doesn't tend to follow rational lines of thought. What do you do when tomorrow's troubles bleed into today's troubles? What do you do when the troubles of today are so intricately connected to the troubles of tomorrow and yesterday and the next ten weeks? What do you do when you feel this and don't seem to be able to stop?

You ask, "How long?"

Sometimes, like the psalmist, we ask "How long?" again and again. And you only ask "How long" when you are overwhelmed. You ask "How long" when you just want the circumstances or the feeling to end but have no power yourself to bring it about. This is where we find David in Psalm 13. Maybe it's where you find yourself as you read this chapter.

It is important to say at the outset that this chapter will not be dealing with the clear medical diagnosis of anxiety/depression that often is helped by medication If you live and love fully, anxiety will hit you at some point, and that's what we are thinking about here. I will be talking about it primarily from an experiential perspective, not as a practitioner. There is a type of anxiety that is deeper and chronic, and for such sufferers, a combination of medication and therapy, as well as community and prayer, might be most helpful. But this is best left up to a medical professional.

I want in this chapter to think about the more everyday experience of anxiety—but I hope that this psalm can speak into your situation, however deep the anxiety may be.

WHEN LIFE ONLY GIVES YOU MORE QUESTIONS

David's distress and anxiety in this psalm seem to be owing to a certain circumstance: namely, his enemies winning over him (v 2). But the psalm is addressed "To the choirmaster," so it is for the entire congregation of Israel to sing. They are not to read themselves out of it and neither should we.

David is pretty bold in his complaint here. This is helpful for us as we process our own complaints before God because often we are shy when it comes to our anxieties, since we think Christians shouldn't feel this way (which gives us something else to be anxious about...) Do you, like David, question God in your anxiety and distress—but then feel guilty about it? We wouldn't have been given this song in Scripture if it weren't appropriate to sing this way. So take heart, anxious Christian. And let's get singing.

David doesn't begin with God's character as he has done

in other psalms. He doesn't begin with his own requests. He doesn't even begin with truth at all. He begins with questions. He begins with confusion. He begins with wondering what on earth is going on in his life.

- He feels forgotten (v 1).
- He feels as if God has hidden his face from him (v 1).
- He feels anxious, wrestling with his thoughts (v 2).
- He feels sorrow (v 2).
- He feels he has been treated unfairly by his enemies (v 2).

Take any one of these feelings on its own and it would be too much to handle. Add them all together and we feel the emotional onslaught that David's questions bring. He goes to the God he trusts, but who, he feels, has forgotten him. He questions God, asking him to show up. David is teaching us that it is good and right to say what we feel. God is inviting us to be honest with him. How do you feel? Tell God. He knows, and he cares.

The pastor Sinclair Ferguson offers encouragement to the woman who is questioning God in anxiety-ridden distress:

> *"Just listen to what your soul is saying. Although you feel that God has deserted you, you know you haven't been, or you would never still be addressing him. When it looks as though faith has collapsed, faith is beginning to be operated."*
>
> *(resources.thegospelcoalition.org/library/ has-god-forgotten-me, accessed 2/25/19)*

There is a shred of faith left, sister, in your questions before God. They are not a sign of faithlessness but of faith. He is keeping you while you walk through the storm.

MAKING BOLD REQUESTS

After boldly questioning God, David moves on to equally bold requests.

Consider and answer me, O LORD my God;
light up my eyes, lest I sleep the sleep of death,
lest my enemy say, "I have prevailed over him,"
lest my foes rejoice because I am shaken. (v 3-4)

Some translations say, "Look on me" or "Listen to me." David wants God not just to make his distress stop, but to actually hear him. Because this is poetry, David uses hyperbole in verse 3 to show how passionate and desperate he is for God to show up. God has promised David, as the obedient king that he has appointed, that his enemies will not prevail over him (Psalm 2)—so here, David is requesting from God what God has promised to him.

There was a moment, about nine months after my fourth son was born, when my body just gave out on me. I had already spent more days in a bed than I ever thought I would, and the prospect of spending more days in a bed away from my kids was more than I could handle. The flood of anxiety over the upheaval it caused them was crushing. As I lay on the floor in extreme physical pain, I saw their scared faces, and I cried out again to God: "Please, God, make it stop." I wrote this note in my phone:

I need God to heal me. And not just for physical
healing, but for my entire family. I want to invest in
my kids. I want to have time with them. They miss
me. I miss them. I want our family to be together
so we can teach our children the truths of God's
word together. But we can't right now. God, answer
according to who you are. It's good for families to
enjoy each other. It's good to enjoy this world and
the people you have given us. You are stripping me
of what matters to me. I know that. But let me
re-emerge refined and with right perspectives and
motives for your glory and my family's good.

In the midst of the physical pain and the emotional anxiety over what this was doing to my kids, I was directing my argument to God. I was making an appeal to him based on who he said he would be. I was making an appeal to him based on what he said was good and right.

Sometimes when we pray, we over-spiritualize things. We pray "according to God's will" but are afraid to actually tell him what we think we need. We caveat our prayers, never wanting anyone to think that our suffering is leading us to unbelief. I think there is a time for us to lay down our requests and bow in contented trust before the Lord. But there is also a time for us to make bold requests of him. Sure, we aren't David—we are not the messianic king. But we are God's people, seeking to live lives that reflect him to a watching world. Praying for deliverance is not a bad thing. Praying for God to give you things he says are good is not a bad thing. While suffering is to be expected in this life, and while God works for our good through our suffering (Romans 8 v 28), he is our Father, and he takes no pleasure in his children being riddled with anxiety and pain. His plan for his people has always been wholeness, not brokenness.

So to pray for deliverance from the brokenness of this world is a good and right prayer, and one we should pray in faith. It doesn't necessarily mean we will be healed in an instant, or at all in this life. We cannot demand that. But it is good to desire it and to ask for it.

BANKING ON A FUTURE HOPE
But we also must all come to a crossroads in our anxiety. There will come a point when the requests have been made and we have said all there is to say. What do we do then? Throw up our hands and say, "God can't be trusted"? Or trust him anyway? In verses 5-6, David looks at the circum-

stances around him and looks up to heaven with tear-filled eyes, saying in effect what Peter said to the Lord in John 6 v 68: "To whom shall we go? You have the words of eternal life." The anxiety has not yet left David. The darkness has not yet lifted. But he knows every other solution to his difficulty will be found wanting. So he resolves to trust and hope in God, based on his promises and his character:

> *But I have trusted in your steadfast love;*
> *my heart shall rejoice in your salvation.*
> *I will sing to the LORD,*
> *because he has dealt bountifully with me.*
>
> *(Psalm 13 v 5-6)*

Notice that the psalm doesn't say that he is delivered. His heart "shall rejoice" in God's salvation—it's future-oriented. There is often no quick fix to anxiety. "When will it end?" we ask through tears. But here David is making a choice to trust before the outcome has happened. He's believing before he sees. This is not prosperity-gospel theology. This is not "name it and claim it," where we demand God give us what he has not promised to. This is believing in what is already certain, in what has already been accomplished, in what is as good as done—in what has been promised. For however God answers our prayers, and however long we struggle now, we do know that one day anxiety shall give way to rejoicing, when we enter our eternal life.

There are countless things that are not certain. We may not get that job. We may not be cured of cancer. We may not have a happy marriage or even get married. We may not see that family member again. These are not promised to us. We cannot bank on them. And if we focus on these things alone, then our anxiety will only grow. Conversely, if we focus on what is promised to us, then those anxiety-inducing unknowns start to reduce in size. Jesus is preparing a place for us (John 14 v 2). Jesus will work all things for good (Romans 8 v 28). We do have a fixed future hope (1 Peter 1 v 3-6). All wrongs will one day be made right (1 Corinthians 15 v 24-28). Our salvation is secure and certain because of what Christ accomplished (John 10 v 28-30). Look at these certainties, as David did, and you will find there is less cause to be anxious about the unknowns, and more reason to rejoiced in what are, for the Christian, the "knowns."

Anxiety is always ready to dog our tracks with "what ifs" and "yes, buts." But we have an answer to it. Dale Ralph Davis speaks of…

> "… the unguessable and lavish friendliness of Yahweh, with which He pledges to dog your tracks all your days … Just to be assured of unfailing love makes all the difference." (Slogging Along in the Paths of Righteousness, pages 22-23)

Anxiety might be asking you what you'll do if your most valuable earthly things are ripped from your hands, or how you would cope if you lost or never gained what you seem to most need. And I can't promise you that those things won't happen. But nothing can take God's covenant faithfulness from you. Let that certainty grow to dwarf the uncertainties of this life. That's what can keep you when the tornado of anxiety menaces on the horizon. That's what will ground you when the winds are howling around you. God, not anxiety, will "dog your tracks all your days."

Knowing this might not change your circumstances. But it does secure your future. And it changes how you feel.

Extra Psalms: Psalms 53, 64 (these psalms deal with circumstances that often lead to anxiety)

Journaling

FEARING DEATH
PSALM 116

I will walk before the LORD
in the land of the living.

Psalm 116 v 9

I spent most of my life basically unaware of death and completely unaffected by death. I didn't go to a single funeral until I was in college, and even then it was for a kid I didn't know.

But all of that changed when we lost our first baby and our third baby, and almost lost our sixth baby. In a matter of moments, my unborn son's life—and mine—were on a knife-edge. And I've never been the same.

Now death no longer feels far off. Now it feels too close for comfort. Now I'm always aware that even my next breath isn't guaranteed.

Since tasting the fragility of life, I've had to wrestle with a lot of questions. How do I live when death is always around the corner? How do I cope with the reality of death? How can life be enjoyed when it can be snuffed out in an instant?

In the years since, I've met people like me—people young and old, who have stared death in the face and then lived to tell the tale. I've met family members who walked through health traumas with their loved one. Instead of being the one on death's brink, they were the one who got the phone call. I've met people who have walked with friends through the death of their child. They didn't bury their own child, but they lost their innocence in that dark valley. I've met people who, like me, spent weeks or months in the hospital and are forever changed by the memory of the constant beeping of machines reminding them of the fragility of their life. And I've met people who, for no apparent reason, woke up one morning with the coldly-gripping realization "One day I will die" and couldn't shake it off.

The overarching feeling all those people have in common is fear. Death was once a distant reality—something talked about as a possibility but which had never really come near. But once it's crouching at your door, it becomes your constant adversary, taunting you with the horrors to come. Author Russ Ramsey says:

"Few things sweep away the clutter of our fears like coming face to face with our own mortality. When this happens, life gets simple in a hurry." (Struck, page 59)

It's true. Dealing with our mortality has a way of simplifying life and showing you what matters. But it also has a way of paralyzing you to the point that you can't even take care of any of those simple things that do matter.

Psalm 116 offers great hope to the one who fears death. It gives a promise: not a promise that death can be avoided but that you will "walk before the LORD in the land of the living" (v 9)—on both sides of death. If you need to live in light of this promise, Psalm 116 is for you.

A PSALM OF DELIVERANCE
Psalm 116 comes on the heels of a great deliverance. It's part of the *Hallel* psalms, which were the songs sung by Israel

as they celebrated Passover and other feasts and festivals. Charles Spurgeon says that this psalm "must in some measure be interpreted in connection with the coming out of Egypt" (*The Treasury of David*, page 66). So this psalm has deliverance from spiritual and physical death in view.

The Israelites knew what it was to live near death constantly. At the Passover, the firstborn sons of Israel were saved ("passed over") from the angel of death because of the blood of lambs on their doorposts. This deliverance must have been forever etched in their minds: they must have remembered holding their sons in safety, even as they heard the wailing of Egyptian mothers and fathers who had not painted any lamb's blood on their doors. As the Israelites crossed the Red Sea hours later, they were shown one more time that death is real, as they walked through on dry land but watched even more Egyptians perish when the waters came rushing back down.

When you are delivered, you can be left paralyzed by fear. We see this in verses 1-11 as the psalmist alternates between praising God and recalling his experiences. It's almost as if the psalmist is saying, *I almost died. I was so close to falling over the edge in my distress. But you saved me! But I almost died, and in my anguish I almost slipped. But you saved me! You are a good and faithful God! But I almost died...* I know that oscillation from the mountaintop (I'm alive) to the valley (I almost died) and back.

Have you experienced this? The memory can't hurt you anymore, but it's not exactly gone either. In the remembering, the psalmist feels what he was delivered from.

- "The snares of death encompassed me; the pangs of Sheol laid hold on me" (v 3).
- "You have delivered my soul from death, my eyes from tears, my feet from stumbling" (v 8).
- "I am greatly afflicted" (v 10).

But this man is not left just to his memories of how near he came to death. He can also remember God's character.

- God hears the cries of his afflicted people (v 1-2).
- His name is sufficient to call on in our distress (v 4).
- He is gracious and merciful and righteous (v 5).
- He preserves the simple and he saves (v 6).
- His presence is with us in the land of the living (v 9).

In the middle of the all the back-and-forth, the psalmist re-members that not only is he delivered but he can rest in that deliverance:

> *Return, O my soul, to your rest;*
> *for the LORD has dealt bountifully with you. (v 7)*

These markers of God's deliverance help us rest as well. Sleep is hard to come by after trauma. The minute your body begins to wind down at the end of the day, your mind is wound up by the memories. Once I was home and safe, I remember that rest was the thing I needed most but the thing I couldn't quite get. My brain wouldn't let me return to normal, to resting, even to sleeping. I needed this verse over and over again: *Return, Courtney, to your rest. See how much God has delivered you already, and rest in him.* When the "snares of death" linger long after the deliverance, this verse is a soft pillow on which to lay your fearful head.

THE PSALMIST'S RESPONSE TO DELIVERANCE

In response to all of this care from the Lord, what do you do? The psalmist knows he can't repay the Lord (v 12), so he does what all delivered people in the psalms do—praises (v 13-14):

> *I will lift up the cup of salvation*
> *and call on the name of the LORD,*
> *I will pay my vows to the LORD*
> *in the presence of all his people.*

Remember, this psalm was sung at the Passover, the festival in which Israel recalled the truth that the only way to escape death is by the blood of another—and so we need to call on the Lord and trust the Lord and cast ourselves on his mercy. The psalmist can render nothing to the Lord for all the benefits God has given him, except to live like those benefits are true. When you know that you have received so much from the Lord, it changes how you live in the land of the living.

But then we reach a confusing verse in this psalm:

> *Precious in the sight of the LORD*
> *is the death of his saints. (v 15)*

After a string of verses telling us how great deliverance from death is, we have a verse that tells us that a believer's death is precious in God's eyes. How can the psalmist say this?

It is because "the land of the living" (v 9) is both a present land and a future land. The psalmist is looking on the goodness of the Lord in this land of the living, but he can know, as we can know, that he will look on the goodness of the Lord fully, finally, and forever in the future land of the living (Revelation 21). This is why the death of the saints is precious in God's eyes. It's the deliverance we are all longing for—not from death but through death. As scary as my brush with death was, the deliverance I received is only a beautiful foretaste of what is to come. One day, I will live in the place Jesus has prepared for me in the eternal land of the living (John 14 v 2). You will too. Psalm 116 is a great song of deliverance for Israel, but for those of us in Christ, it's a song we can sing all the louder. Even though we die, we will live (John 11 v 25).

LET DEATH'S REALITY CHANGE HOW YOU LIVE
In the final four verses, our psalmist comes to a joyous conclusion. He will be God's servant (Psalm 116 v 16). He will bring his sacrifice of thanksgiving (v 17). He will pay vows

to the Lord in the presence of the people (v 18). And he will praise the Lord (v 19). The psalm begins and ends with a commitment to lifelong devotion to the Lord because of his deliverance of the psalmist. He has not been left unchanged by his deliverance. How could he be?

Looking closely at death and living to tell others about it should change our priorities. Yes, it's hard to live with the fear of death hanging over you, but it also lets you live for the only thing that truly matters—the God who delivers you from death. I feel like I got a second chance at living. It was incredibly re-orienting. It changed how I parent, how I write, how I view success, how I view what matters, how I worship. I want my life to count for something and not be wasted. Yes, my life can end in an instant, but until then I want to live like every moment is my last, for the glory of the God who is wonderfully sovereign over life and death.

For the psalmist, deliverance looked like coming out of Egypt. For us it might mean surviving an illness, a car accident, or a traumatic birth. But for both him and us, supremely it means passing from mortal life into eternal life. That is the hope. While we live, we serve God and worship him fully. When we die, our death is precious because our greatest obstacle has been defeated—sin.

Psalm 116 v 9 became a verse that was dear to me during those long days in the hospital. "I will walk before the Lord in the land of the living." I wanted to know—and I was able to know—that life could be found on the other side of that operating room, whether on earth or in heaven. Death seems so final. It's awful. It's painful. It's frightening. But in my moments of greatest fear, I could know that God had dealt bountifully with me by dealing with my greatest barrier to life—my own sin. I could know that physical death could never take away the eternal life promised to me in Christ.

For those who trust Christ, we've all been delivered from

death. We will all one day walk in the land of the living, even if sometimes the prospect of getting there is utterly terrifying. After a brush with death, we may still feel overwhelmed, but we can ultimately rest and praise the One who delivered us. And of course this applies not only to those of us who have nearly died but to all of us who have been saved. We will not ultimately escape physical death, but after we have closed our eyes on this life, we will open them in the presence of the Lord, in the final and best land of the living. There is nothing to fear. We have been saved and should respond to God together in praise.

One of my favorite books to read with my kids is *Dangerous Journey*, a children's version of John Bunyan's *Pilgrim's Progress*. The hero, Christian, walks through one last trial before he reaches heaven's shores, and as he feels the waters of death rising to his head, he is scared. He has to pass through the River of Death if he is to get to the other side and reach heaven's gates. But the process is horrible—terrifying. As the waters continue to rise, the book says:

> *"But the troubles a man goes through in these waters are no sign that God has forsaken him. All at once the sun was visible through the mist. The pilgrims felt new strength within themselves, the water became less deep, the ground was firmer underfoot. And so they reached the shore." (page 109)*

It gets me every time.

You and I know the One who pronounced himself the resurrection and the life. Death is real, but there is no need to fear. Our souls can be at rest—even through death. We will walk before the Lord in the land of the living, both in this life and the one to come.

Extra Psalms: Psalms 18, 30, 90, 118

Journaling

SUSTAINED
PSALM 66

Come and hear, all you who fear God,
and I will tell you what he has done for my
soul.

Psalm 66 v 16

It had been a long, hard journey to reach this place. She had lost everything back when she thought she had the rest of her life to live. In an instant, she had gone from devoted wife and mother to a woman bereft of everyone she'd ever loved. She had rebelled, shaking her fist at the God whom she had once loved. She had wandered. She had been destitute. She hadn't been able to see how God would work for her.

And then she had been lovingly brought back by the very God she had rejected in her grief.

She knew what it meant to be alone, to be hungry, without a home, without a family.

She knew what it meant to be bitter. But she also knew what it meant to be delivered. She knew what it meant to be sustained.

HE HAS NOT LEFT YOU

Naomi, in the book of Ruth, is a woman whom we often talk about in negative terms. "Don't be like her. Don't rebel. Don't grow bitter. Don't take matters into your own hands."

But she was also a woman who could testify to God's sustaining work in her life even when it seemed all hope was gone. She was a woman who was not only kept by God but was also included in the great storyline of Scripture—the lineage of King David, and ultimately Jesus the Messiah.

Naomi lived in a time when "there was no king in Israel. Everyone did what was right in his own eyes" (Judges 21 v 25). In keeping with that approach to life, when food ran short her family left God's land and went to Moab (subtext: not God's land). There, she lost her husband, her sons, and all she had. But she gained Ruth (her daughter-in-law) and, having returned to Israel and benefited from the kindness of her relative Boaz, she eventually gained an heir to pass on the family name.

By the end of the short book that bears Ruth's name, Naomi had come full circle: "the women said to Naomi, 'Blessed be the LORD, who has not left you this day without a redeemer ... He shall be to you a restorer of life and a nourisher of your old age'" (Ruth 4 v 14,-15). And so I imagine that Naomi could sing the words of Psalm 66: "Come and hear, all you who fear God, and I will tell you what he has done for my soul" (v 16). I imagine many of you can as well.

Psalm 66 is a psalm of thanksgiving: one sung back to God on the heels of a great deliverance. It's one of many thanksgiving psalms. The psalmist speaks of a deliverance in the past and a deliverance in the present. And because of all that God has done, he feels something. He feels sustained. He feels carried. He feels that God is bearing him up, carrying the burden for him.

This psalm breaks into five sections:
1. Worship God for what he has done (v 1-4).
2. God's power extends to the past and to all the earth (v 5-8).
3. God's power extends to us personally, especially in suffering and trial (v 10-12).
4. God's power displayed elicits a response (v 13-15).
5. God's power displayed invites others to learn (v 16-20).

In every section, we see God sustaining the psalmist. His power is everywhere. While we will may not have experienced the exact same deliverance, since this is a song addressed "To the choirmaster," it is meant to be sung by God's people as a whole. If we are in Christ, we can say along with the psalmist that we are sustained by the awesome deeds of the Lord. And sometimes—even in times when our earthly circumstances suggest that we should be afraid/insecure—we can see a specific instance when God has delivered us, carried us, sustained us. This psalm enables us to know what to do with those moments and those feelings.

YOUR DELIVERANCE SHOULD MAKE YOU *FEEL*

The overarching theme of the psalms of thanksgiving is one of praise. There is something wrong if we get our prayers answered, only to respond with muted joy. We would wonder if they had been truly fervent in their prayers if someone responded to God's help with indifference or lack of any emotion. Remember the words of Naomi's friends:

> *Blessed be the LORD, who has not left you this day without a redeemer, and may his name be renowned in Israel! He shall be to you a restorer of life and a nourisher of your old age, for your daughter-in-law who loves you, who is more to you than seven sons, has given birth to him. (Ruth 4 v 14-15)*

The psalmist says the same thing.

> *Shout for joy to God, all the earth;*
> *sing the glory of his name;*
> *give to him glorious praise!*
> *Say to God, "How awesome are your deeds!*
> *So great is your power that your enemies come*
> *cringing to you.*
> *All the earth worships you*
> *and sings praises to you;*
> *they sing praises to your name. Selah.*
>
> *(Psalm 66 v 1-4)*

The deliverance the psalmist experienced is so great that he calls not just his friends to praise but the entire earth! God is the only God of the nations and the only God of the creation. And, as the following verses show, his power over creation and in history is what leads the psalmist to feel sustained. God works in every corner of the world that he has made, and all of us should praise him for that.

The psalmist begins with praise before he even says why he is praising God. It's as if he can't contain his excitement in shouting *Praise the Lord!* When we get good gifts from God that we've asked for (or even that we haven't asked for!), God should be the immediate object of our praise. He did it. He displayed his power. His name is great. Praise the Lord. These words are the shout of one who feels safe, who feels loved, who feels cared for by God. And that is what we feel when we realize that God has delivered us. We feel sustained.

YOUR DELIVERANCE AND *THE* DELIVERANCE

While the psalmist doesn't reveal the specifics of his deliverance, he connects it to a greater deliverance that would have been understood by all of Israel:

Come and see what God has done:
he is awesome in his deeds toward the children
of man.
He turned the sea into dry land;
they passed through the river on foot.
There did we rejoice in him,
who rules by his might forever,
whose eyes keep watch on the nations—
let not the rebellious exalt themselves. Selah. (v 5-8)

When did God turn the sea into dry land? When did his people pass through that river on foot? In Exodus 14, when Israel was delivered from Egypt by crossing the Red Sea on foot, when the Egyptian army perished behind them. And then in Joshua 3, when, after forty years of wilderness wandering, Israel crossed the River Jordan on foot, God having stopped up the waters, and so entered the promised land.

Why bring this up? Here is a psalm about God sustaining a person, so why bring up the nation's history? Because our personal salvation is always connected to the larger body of God's covenant people. We are never saved in isolation from what God is doing corporately—and all our specific deliverances in this life should point us back to the greater deliverance of our life. The Red Sea and River Jordan crossings were part of the greatest historic event in the life of Israel, when God rescued them from slavery and brought them into the promised land. It was the greatest example of God sustaining his people through danger and lack and failings. And every other deliverance after that foundational deliverance hearkened them back to remember and praise God for his sustaining power.

Isn't that true for us as well? Every personal deliverance is a call to remember our greatest deliverance in Christ. Every time we realize God has answered our prayers, it is a call back to his abundant faithfulness in Christ. He hears us and answers us because of what Christ accomplished for us. We are always connected to the larger deliverance.

EVEN IN SUFFERING, HE IS NOT FAR OFF

The overarching theme is that God is the One sustaining it all. He is over the deliverance, but he is also over the difficulties. Israel knew that God was the One who led them to being trapped on the edge of the Red Sea, as well as the One who delivered them through it (Exodus 14 v 1-2, 30-31). So it was in the individual lives of God's people (Psalm 66 v 10-11). As it had been for Naomi, it was a long hard road to the "place of abundance" (v 12).

But here, the purpose of recounting of suffering is different than in lament psalms. In a psalm of lament we are getting the account of suffering in real time. In this psalm, we're looking back on what happened. It doesn't diminish what happened. But it focuses on the experience not of the hardship but of God showing up to sustain, to deliver, and to restore. It was only on the other side of the trials that the psalmist could get any perspective on what had happened.

Isn't that the case with us? It's hard to discern what God is doing in the midst of everything. When all we see are crushing burdens, walls closing in, enemies on every side, death crouching at the door, pain that is too much to bear, or even a faith that is slipping, we can't always see that it's God who is holding it all together and doing so in a way that is always good. We cannot, as Spurgeon put it, "trace his hand"— but sometimes, I don't think we are meant to. The psalmist praises like this because he is on the other side and has seen God's purifying purposes in his suffering (v 10). The real test is if we come out on the other side still praising God and ready to see what he has been doing and in us, not that we can perfectly discern God's purposes in the midst of it.

RESPOND AND INVITE

The rest of the psalm is a beautiful picture of what it looks like to be sustained by the Lord. The psalmist concludes the psalm as he opened it, with a response of praise and devotion:

> *I will come into your house with burnt offerings;*
> *I will perform my vows to you,*
> *that which my lips uttered*
> *and my mouth promised when I was in trouble.*
>
> *(v 13-14)*

We need to pause here. When all is good and we've come to the other side of a hard time, we tend to congratulate ourselves. Our marriage is saved, or a work project is turned around and garners praise and profit, or our depression lifts, or a ministry that was once failing suddenly grows, or our child's problems cease and the pressures in family life turn to pleasures, and we look at our bright horizons and marvel at our strength. You might not say it out loud, of course—I don't—but I know that inwardly I have been tempted to pat myself on the back when I've made it through a tough time. And even if we acknowledge that God has had a hand in sustaining us through that time, we can be like those lepers whom Jesus healed, but who walked away to enjoy their deliverance and didn't turn back to praise or thank him (Luke 17 v 11-19).

Here is the challenge: if we don't respond with an uncontainable thankfulness to God for sustaining us through difficulty, then we are showing that we take God's sustaining of us for granted (as if we deserve it), or that deep down we think we sustained ourselves (as if we did it).

And if that's your temptation, as it is mine, we could do far worse than recite aloud verses 16-19 of Psalm 66:

Come and hear, all you who fear God,
  and I will tell what he has done for my soul.
I cried to him with my mouth,
  and high praise was on my tongue.
If I had cherished iniquity in my heart,
  the LORD would not have listened.
But truly God has listened;
  he has attended to the voice of my prayer

The right response to God sustaining us is not to would marvel in our newfound circumstances but to marvel at God and his care—and then tell others about it. Every deliverance you face is a call for this kind of outward praise that prompts corporate praise. When God does what you've asked for (or have given up asking for, or have even never thought of asking for in the first place!), the right response is always to tell all who will hear, "Come and listen to what God has done for me." Your deliverance is for others. It's for us. It's for God's glory.

So when we see how we have been sustained, we shout for joy to God, praise God, bless God. He has not left us. He has not forgotten us. He has not failed us. He has sustained us. We can say with the psalmist, "He has not removed his steadfast love from me." You are sustained. Praise him!

Extra Psalms: Psalms 3, 62, 91, 121

Journaling

STUCK IN MY FAITH
PSALM 119

If your law had not been my delight,
I would have perished in my affliction.

Psalm 119 v 92

The enthusiasm of new Christians tends to be contagious to be around—they have zeal, curiosity, joy, and energy. We've all met people who've just become Christians, and it's changed everything about them. We've all met the woman for whom life has gone from black and white to a sea of amazing color. She wants to read. She wants to study Scripture. She wants to talk about God to anyone who will listen. Perhaps you remember when that woman was you.

And then some time passes. Old sin patterns re-emerge. Bible truths don't jump off the page at her anymore. Suffering comes, and it's harder to walk by the word when darkness clouds her way. Even in church, the worshipful feelings she had during the singing are gone. She is stuck. What was once new and exciting is now normal and routine. And maybe today that woman is you.

This is where Psalm 119 comes in.

Even the most fervent believers get stuck sometimes, because life is hard and this world is broken. The zeal of your early Christian days might be waning, but Psalm 119 speaks to you words of encouragement: you aren't the first or the last to feel stuck in your walk with the Lord.

We often see Psalm 119 as being a psalm about delighting in the word, and it is; but the reality for many of us is that sometimes we don't delight in the word we claim to love. The psalmist spends a lot of time asking for delight in the word that he declares worthy of admiration:

> Oh that my ways may be steadfast
> in keeping your statutes! (v 5)

Sometimes we pray verse 5 in the hope that our love will come back. But what do you do when it doesn't? What do you do when you are left waiting for your prayer for desire to be answered? Psalm 119 comes to the stuck person with the thing they once loved—the word—and then lets them linger there a while. In this extra-long psalm (the longest chapter in the Bible), we get hope for when we feel stuck in our faith, not necessarily because it tells us what to do to get out of that rut but because it takes us back to the basics— reminding us again and again that God's word is good. (For an entire book on this, try, for example, *His Testimonies, My Heritage*, ed. Kristie Anyabwile.) The theme of this psalm is that God's word is for our good.

SANCTIFICATION TAKES TIME (SO SOMETIMES WE GET STUCK)

There are a lot of verses in Psalm 119—176 to be exact. And its 22 sections are composed as an acrostic of the Hebrew alphabet. The commentator Dale Ralph Davis, in speaking of another passage of Scripture that also uses the Hebrew alphabet poetically (the book of Lamentations), says that sometimes it takes the entire Hebrew alphabet to get hope in suffering (sermonaudio.com/sermoninfo.asp?SID=42317195399, accessed 7/6/19). The principle applies here as well. Being stuck can soon feel like a lifetime of waiting or wading—like reading a 176-verse chapter in the Bible. Sanctification—becoming like Jesus—is messy, is hard, and takes a long time. Growth in God's word is not an overnight success. Sometimes it takes the entire Hebrew alphabet for God to finish what he starts. But he will (Philippians 1 v 6).

Some psalms find their resolution in a few verses, but the writer of Psalm 119 feels the weight of waiting as much as we feel the weight of reading it. It must have taken a long time to write, but sometimes it takes a long time for the word to become a delight again. Through it all we get glimpses of the psalmist's conviction that God's word is precious to him, so he perseveres. He keeps plugging away at the writing and waiting and wading, because he's certain that there is no other resolution to how he feels.

This message—that God does act, though often we have to wait—is one we see all throughout Scripture. Here is just one example:

For still the vision awaits its appointed time; it
hastens to the end—it will not lie. If it seems slow,
wait for it; it will surely come; it will not delay.
(Habakkuk 2 v 3)

Habakkuk was waiting on a word from the Lord, for God to act in the lives of his rebellious people and in judgment on his enemies. And Habakkuk displays trust. He knows that God will work; he will speak through his word and effect change.

So with us. God will work. He will get us "unstuck." Growth will happen in a believer, and being stuck will not be your defining marker—though it may take time. But… how do we *know* that God will change us? How can we be certain? Because Jesus doesn't leave his blood-bought people to fend for themselves. He gave us the Holy Spirit, and if the Holy Spirit is living in you and you are therefore united to Christ through his finished work on the cross, you can trust that he is at work in you today, even if it is undetectable to you. Jesus will finish the work he starts in us. Our sanctification is a done deal.

So what if you can't see it? This is where we need to lean on our church community. We might not be able to see how the word is working in us, but that is one reason why God has given us a fellowship of other believers: to help us see the ways God is working in us, even when we feel stuck. All through the New Testament, we see examples of the apostles Paul and Peter and other writers identifying evidences of God's grace in the life of those they are writing to. Just think of the Corinthian church for a moment. There didn't look to be much to commend. They were condoning immorality, were abusing the Lord's table, and were divided and choosing sides. They seemed pretty stuck. Yet Paul began his first letter to them with praise and thanksgiving for Christ's work in their lives (1 Corinthians 1 v 4-9). Part of what it means to live in community with other believers is to spur each other on to greater holiness; and sometimes we do that by identifying ways in which others are already growing more like Jesus. But we also do that by telling them how that growth can continue (as Paul does in most of the other 15 ½ chapters of 1 Corinthians!) So if you feel stuck, and, like the psalmist, you want the word to be your delight and to have a transforming effect, ask a trusted Christian friend (or your spouse) to show you how that is already the case in your life. Let another person be your eyes to see this work in your life.

THE WORD REALLY IS WHAT YOU NEED

But that leads to the next question. How does the slow process of sanctification happen?

When I was a kid, my dad had me read Psalm 119 and circle every instance of God's word mentioned in the psalm. His point? To show me how important the word is by getting me into the word. Nearly every verse mentions some variation of God's word: instruction, law, or truth. It is a psalm about the far-reaching impact of God's word in the life of a believer. Psalm 119 shows us that the way we get unstuck is by the word doing its work in our life. No matter our circumstances, no matter our feelings, no matter our stage of growth, we need the word. It is as simple as that.

Why do we need this word? Let's look at two pictures of the word from Psalm 119.

*Your word is a lamp to my feet
and a light to my path. (v 105)*

This is a very well-known verse in a well-known psalm. Seen in its cultural context, it becomes even more precious. At that time a lamp was all you had to light your path in the dark of night. There was no electricity or flashlight on your phone. So to compare God's word to a lamp that lights your way in darkness is to show us the incomparable value that God's word has for our everyday lives. Without it you can't see anything. Without it, everything is pitch black with no discernible way forward. But with it, you can see. With it, you know in which direction you are going—and you can grow.

Life can be disorienting at times. Even though I live with physical light all around me, there have been instances in my life where I have felt bleak darkness in my soul. At these times I don't know whom to trust. I don't know how to understand my circumstances. I don't know how to move forward. But somehow, in some way, the word gives me light. It reminds me of the sure outcome for this broken world. It gives me a right perspective. And it is a lamp to my feet.

Only when the word lights your path can you say with the psalmist, "It is good for me that I was afflicted, that I might learn your statutes" (v 71). That's the word doing its work, lighting the way even in the darkness.

> *How sweet are your words to my taste,*
> *sweeter than honey to my mouth! (v 103)*

I love a good meal with friends. I love the sweetness of ice cream, the richness of pasta, and the spice of Tex-Mex (my favorite). But what I love most is experiencing it with others. I love tasting the food and then talking about how much I love the experience of it. Meditating on God's word day and night is an experience like this—but better. It is not just that the word is spiritually nutritious but that the word is spiritually sweet. The psalmist has experienced what God's word does to a person's soul—how it heightens his desire for more—and he is exclaiming about that to all who will listen. Much as a good meal makes us want to recommend it to others, the sweet feast of God's word causes us to invite all to come, taste, and see the sweetness of the word—and that, in turn, heightens our own enjoyment of it.

In nearly every stanza, the psalmist makes his case that the word is what we need in order to grow—to get unstuck. It lights our path in darkness. It is better than the best meal with friends. It's everything.

YOU CAN'T DO IT, BUT GOD CAN

The psalm begins with a promise:

> *Blessed are those whose way is blameless,*
> *who walk in the law of the LORD!*
> *Blessed are those who keep his testimonies,*
> *who seek him with their whole heart. (v 1-2)*

And it ends (almost) with a plea:

Let my cry come before you, O LORD;
  give me understanding according to your word!
Let my plea come before you;
  deliver me according to your word. (v 169-170)

But before the psalmist finishes comes the reality. After all these prayers, we might expect a triumphant resolution, but…

I have gone astray like a lost sheep; seek your servant,
  for I do not forget your commandments. (v 176)

He doesn't end particularly hopeful! He has gone astray, after he has just spent 176 verses saying he doesn't want to go astray. And isn't that life? Isn't that the process of growing in holiness? You make progress, only to fall backwards. You kill a particular sin, only to be met with a new one. Hence we feel spiritually stuck. If Psalm 119 feels like a long trek up a mountain, it's because the Christian life is like that. We are striving upwards, but it takes a lot of hard work to get to the top—but reaching the peak is worth it.

And as we go to work, we find that God is at work (Philippians 2 v 12-13). Notice who the "seeker" is as this psalm ends (Psalm 119 v 176). It's God. In the end, the psalmist understands that the only way he will get out of feeling stuck is if God seeks him out. And God does. He seeks his lost sheep. He brings us back to the right path. He continues to work growth in us. As we read the word and cry out to him for more desire, we can rest in the knowledge that he will reach out to us even more. He will bring us all the way to glory. If it was all left on our shoulders, we would be helpless and exhausted. But when we know that God is seeking us, growing us, and keeping us, we can have the strength and confidence to press on and keep coming back to him in his word.

THE PLACE TO START, THE PLACE TO STAY

Our family song is the now-popular hymn "He Will Hold Me Fast," and I can't help but want to sing this as I read the last part of Psalm 119: "He'll not let my soul be lost, his promises shall last." Psalm 119's message to the Christian who is stuck in their faith is to keep in the word, or get back into the word. It will work itself into you and grow you. You might meet a Christian who is in the word and still feels stuck; but you will never meet a Christian who is growing well while not reading the word. It's the place to start and it's the place to stay, even if it takes time to get un-stuck. The word is a lamp to your feet. And your feet will move along the path, bit by bit. You're not stuck anymore. You're heading home to God, lit by his word. For he always finishes what he starts, and he's at work in you today.

Extra Psalm: Psalm 19

Journaling

_____
_____
_____
_____
_____
_____
_____
_____
_____
_____
_____
_____
_____
_____
_____
_____
_____
_____
_____
_____
_____
_____

CONTENT
PSALM 131

Lord, my heart is not proud;
my eyes are not haughty.
I do not get involved with things
too great or too wondrous for me.

Psalm 131 v 1 (CSB)

My phrase for the past year has been to "stay in my lane." You are probably familiar with the importance of staying in your lane on the actual road. The boundary markers are there for a reason. They are for your good and the good of society. But on the road, there are many things that can lead us to swerve out of our lane—most notably our tendency towards to be distracted.

I have this same problem in the lane called "my life."

I'm driving down the proverbial road of my own life, and I see a human-interest story on the news and feel compelled to respond (or find a solution to the problem being highlighted). I get distracted. The next thing I know, I'm causing the traffic of my own lane to slow down, and I'm on the verge of an accident. Or I jump on social media, see a new controversy, and feel compelled to respond—not my lane. I see a mom doing something for her children that I can't seem to do for mine, so I feel defeated—not my lane. I have to regularly remind myself that there are specific things God has called me to focus on, and other things he has not. And in many ways, that's a key to my contentment: to "not get involved with things too great or too wondrous for me." The key to contentment is to know that I am not God, and I can't be involved in things outside my pay grade—outside of my lane. It won't end well. Can you relate?

Psalm 131 is, as Charles Spurgeon said, "one of the shortest psalms to read, but one of the longest to learn" (*Treasury of David*, page 136). It is a beautifully short psalm about finding contentment in God alone through staying in your own lane. But it's even more than that. As we lift our gaze off the things that can consume us (and move us out of our lane), we see a path towards trust instead of comparison, and thankfulness instead of jealousy. We learn contentment.

The journey towards contentment takes a lifetime to complete, but we can start that journey now and follow David's path to get there.

THE KEY TO CONTENTMENT

The psalm begins with…

> LORD, *my heart is not proud;*
> *my eyes are not haughty.*
> *I do not get involved with things*
> *too great or too wondrous for me. (v 1a, CSB)*

At the outset, David basically says that the way to be content is to not be proud and to not be jealous. This is a psalm about giving up self-sufficiency, self-focus, and self-worship, and trading it all for a proper view of ourselves in light of God's gracious provision. A proud, arrogant heart will not be content with what God has given. A woman with haughty eyes will constantly be looking around at others with disdain and superiority, viewing what she has (or doesn't have) as owing to her value. This is why Proverbs tells us that haughty eyes are one of the things that God hates (Proverbs 6 v 17). A proud heart and haughty eyes are so clouded by self-focus that they can't see God rightly or desire God truly.

The heart and the eyes are the source of so much of our discontentment—and therefore this is where we start to fight for contentment. David says his heart is not proud, meaning he "is neither proud in his opinion of himself, contemptuous of others, nor self-righteous before the Lord" (Spurgeon, *Treasury of David*, page 136). He sees himself rightly in relation to God and to others. Dealing with his heart helps him deal with his eyes. His "eyes are not raised too high" (v 1)—they are not focused on things outside of his control; and as a result, his eyes are not looking around at what others have, prompting thoughts that he deserves better.

Just think about what happens when your eyes are "raised too high." When you see your friend sharing her new kitchen remodel on Instagram, how does your heart respond? When your neighbor gets a new car, does pride rise up in your heart about all that you deserve instead of her? When you see someone go on the better vacation (or just any vacation), or the engagement ring, or the third pregnancy, do your eyes look beyond your present circumstances and tempt you towards discontentment? Here, David is telling us that the key to fighting that is to deal with our heart and our eyes rightly. We should not let pride make us think we deserve more than what God has graciously given us, and we should not let our eyes gaze more on what others enjoy than on his gracious provision to us.

If our heart is not proud, then we won't be tempted towards jealousy of what others have that we do not. But if we think we deserve better, jealousy is quick to follow. This is where the second half of the verse comes into play, where

David says he doesn't get involved with things "too wondrous" for him. He stays in his lane.

This was what the apostle Peter struggled with. When Jesus forgave and commissioned him, Jesus explained that Peter's path involved him dying in a way Peter would never choose (John 21 v 15-24). Instead of staying in his lane, Peter veered into John's, looking at John and asking his Lord, "What about John?" By all accounts, John was going to live a long life. Peter had been given a death sentence. And how does Jesus reply to Peter's question about John? Essentially, he says, *Mind your own business. You just follow me.* Jesus doesn't give Peter a direct answer to what will happen to John because that's beyond Peter's understanding. Peter's getting involved in things far too high for his finite mind. He needs to focus on his own lane and on his own work given to him by Jesus.

The way to make progress in contentment is to be like David, not like Peter. Know your place in the kingdom, David says. Stay in your lane. Do not be proud, expecting and assuming you deserve better than what God has graciously given. Do not be jealous, seeing what others have and pining to have it yourself. Instead, stay in your lane. The path to contentment includes minding our own business, but it also includes trusting that God knows better than us when it comes to how our life works out. God knows what he is doing, and his plans are "too great and too wondrous" for our finite minds to understand. Maybe we need to memorize Romans 11 v 33-36 and recite it each morning:

> *Oh, the depth of the riches and wisdom and*
> *knowledge of God! How unsearchable are his*
> *judgments and how inscrutable his ways!*
> *"For who has known the mind of the Lord,*
> *or who has been his counselor?"*

"Or who has given a gift to him
that he might be repaid?"
For from him and through him and to him are all
things. To him be glory forever. Amen.

REACHING CONTENTMENT

We've seen how to achieve basic contentment in ordinary life: by focusing on what God has given us rather than demanding or pining for more. But now David tells us how it is possible to remain content even when God's good gifts and provision seem to be absent—even in times of great suffering and pain.

Instead, I have calmed and quieted my soul
like a weaned child with its mother;
my soul is like a weaned child.

(Psalm 131 v 2, CSB)

This verse is set up as a direct contrast to the previous one, where David basically says that he minds his own business. David doesn't concern himself with things beyond his control. Instead of having an inflated view of himself, he compares himself to a weaned child—a contented child.

To grasp his point, we need to pause to consider what a weaned child was like in David's day. In our culture, we tend to think of a weaned child as a young infant, but that was not the case in David's context. In fact, many children weren't weaned until around the age of three, which changes our interpretation of what a weaned soul looks like. The writer Jon Bloom explains it this way:

"In ancient Near Eastern cultures, children weren't
weaned from breastfeeding until at least three years
of age, and sometimes older. By those ages, children's
cognitive and verbal abilities [are] normally quite
developed. This meant that the transition from the

familiar comfort and nourishment of a mother's
breast to no longer receiving such comfort and
nourishment would have been psychologically and
emotionally more difficult than for a younger child.
One can imagine a three-year-old's tears and anger
and insistence and complaints and pleas and repeated
physical attempts to nurse again, only to be denied
by the one person who had up to that point been the
source of such intimate comfort and nourishment.
Why won't Mommy nurse me anymore?"
(desiringgod.org/articles/child-like-humility-
produces-peace, accessed 4/18/19)

One of my children really struggled with weaning. When I approached his first birthday, I knew that weaning was both inevitable and necessary. I needed it. Our family needed it. As much as my son didn't want it, he needed it too.

So we started the process. Little bit by little bit, I dropped feedings. With each dropped feeding, he cried. One moment stands out to me vividly, as the ultimate example of just how hard weaning was for him. He had few words at one year old, but he could say "mama." And as my husband carried him down the stairs, he reached out his arms for me and cried, "Mama! Mama!" What he didn't know was that there was milk waiting for him downstairs, and not just milk but a wonderful breakfast. He would not starve. But his little brain didn't understand that. He wanted the comfort. He needed the comfort.

Psalm 131 gives us the opposite image. Instead of clamoring for milk, the image in Psalm 131 is one of trust—even contentment. When David wants to convey an image of resolute rest and calm, he uses the analogy of a successfully weaned child, which in that culture would have provided a concrete example. Everyone would have understood the effort it took to wean a child. While this seems like a sweet image at first reading, it's really an image that speaks of much struggle. Becoming contented is a fight. From the child weaned of its mother's milk to the adult woman weaned of the world's comforts, we don't come to contentment by default. But when we do reach that point, it's delightful. Everyone would have understood not only the contentment that a weaned child had but also the trust that a weaned child had in its mother. Tim Keller says that this image is the ultimate picture of contentment:

> *"A nursing child, held by its mother, is highly aware of the milk she can offer and will squirm and cry if denied. A child who has been "weaned" (verse 2), however, and no longer nurses, is content to be with its mother, enjoying her closeness and love without wanting anything else." (The Songs of Jesus, page 337)*

The weaned child enjoys their mother for who she is, rather than just for what she gives him or her. We fall into discontentment when we see God only as our gift-giver or the one who delivers us from hard circumstances, and we don't enjoy him for himself. When that's our perspective, losing a gift or entering difficult circumstances must diminish or destroy our contentment. Conversely, the weaned soul, when stripped of the comfort of this world, sees God as the only One worthy of her desire and her trust. She wants him for himself, not for what he can give her.

This is the heart of true contentment. As we see ourselves rightly, "stay in our lane," and trust God as the source of our contentment, rather than what he gives us, we can be content at all times, because our contentment is not contingent on our circumstances. Just as the child's comfort is rooted in its mother (not in what she gives them), our contentment is rooted in God (not in what he gives us).

And contentment is, first and foremost, an internal response: David says, "Like a weaned child is my soul within me" (v 2). The effects of contentment might spill out (just as the effects of discontentment tend to), but most of the time you can never tell who is content and who is not. While our external responses to life might get the most airtime, God is concerned about our hidden responses as well. He sees it all—from our soul to our outward actions.

The weaning process for a child involved great struggle and oftentimes confusion. Comfort is so much more, well, comfortable, isn't it? But like the weaned child, we must learn to trust that the comfort will come sometimes in ways we don't even know are possible.

THE CALL OF THE CONTENTED

After seeing the response of the contented, the last verse makes even more sense.

> *Israel, put your hope in the LORD,*
> *both now and forever. (v 3, CSB)*

Since this psalm takes a lifetime to learn, the corporate call to trust God both now and forever is an apt one. Contentment today might not mean contentment tomorrow, so the call again and again is to trust—to hope in the Lord today, and each day. Like a weaned child trusts that its mother will still be their comfort even when what they love most has dried up, so we can and must trust that God, even in our weaning process, will be our comfort "from this time forth and forevermore" (v 3, ESV).

Only then will we be truly content. Only then will we be able to "stay in our lane" and trust him with whatever else is happening on the road around and ahead of us.

Extra Psalm: Psalm 16

Journaling

GRATEFUL
PSALM 103

Bless the Lord, O my soul,
and forget not all his benefits.

Psalm 103 v 2

We often ask our kids at dinner what one thing from their day they are thankful for. They're young, so you can imagine the range of answers. Sometimes they are thankful for things—a television show or their toys; sometimes for people; sometimes for things that don't make a whole lot of sense to me! Often, they struggle to come up with something because they can't remember the day behind them. In large part that's because of their age, but it's also because the discipline of remembering for the sake of gratitude is exactly that—a discipline. It doesn't always come naturally, for kids or for adults.

Some of us find it hard to feel grateful. Others of us find it easy to feel grateful but maybe aren't grateful for the right things.

Psalm 103 is a call to remember. But it's also a call to gratitude.

DELIVERANCE LEADS TO GRATITUDE

The psalm begins and ends with a call to praise:

> *Bless the LORD, O my soul,*
> *and all that is within me,*
> *bless his holy name! (v 1)*

> *Bless the LORD, all his works,*
> *in all places of his dominion.*
> *Bless the LORD, O my soul! (v 22)*

There is always something to be grateful for. Like my children, we can think of things throughout our days—the meal you shared with a friend, the new book you just received in the mail, the freshly planted flowers, the sunshine or the rain. In all of these things, our feelings of gratitude should be channeled to the Giver of all good things. Since we know there is a Giver, we're to bless the Lord for all the things he gives us.

In her book *Growing in Gratitude: Rediscovering the Joy of a Thankful Heart,* Mary Mohler describes gratitude this way:

> *"It is an intentional mindset that stems from the*
> *fact that since we have indeed received Christ Jesus*
> *the Lord, are walking with him, and are rooted*
> *and established in the faith, we will overflow with*
> *thanksgiving as a result." (page 15)*

To be grateful, we need to notice the good things we're given and then remember them. I have friends who have a "gratitude jar" or a "wall of thankfulness" in their homes. With each answered prayer or reminder of God's care, they write it down and place it in the jar or on the wall. At the end of the year, they read every instance of God's "benefits" towards them. What kind of effect do you think this has on their souls? It's tremendous! David is calling us to remember again and again all that we've been given.

But there are some days when we don't get lunch with a friend, or we have no extra money for that book—days when it rains when we needed sun, or is dry when we hoped for rain. Sometimes you can't think of anything to add to the gratitude jar. Other days, life is going so well that we could fill our prayers with thanks for our daily blessings but forget that there is anything beyond the material and relational joys of our life right now.

At both those times—when life is hard and when life is very good—you need to be reminded of the big-picture benefits that are always true of God's people, and are always to be the greatest fuel for your gratitude:

- He forgives all of your iniquity (v 3a).
- He heals all of your diseases (v 3b).
- He redeems your life from the pit (v 4a).
- He crowns you with steadfast love and mercy (v 4b).
- He satisfies you with good, renewing your youth like the eagle's (v 5).

These are benefits that are true all of the time. When the daily benefits can't be seen (and even when they can), we can keep this long-term vision in view. In Christ, God does forgive your iniquity. In Christ, he does redeem you from the pit. In Christ, he will one day heal you of every disease (and may even heal you in this life). In Christ, he crowns you with steadfast love and mercy. In Christ, he satisfies you with good and gives you renewed energy (like the eagle). He has done these things for you. Are you brimming with gratitude for them yet?

And there's more.

HOW GRATITUDE GROWS
It's as if David can't stop thinking about all the ways that God is good and kind towards him. Gratitude for God's character just flows out.

God doesn't forget those who are oppressed (v 6); instead he is working to execute justice. He has revealed himself to his people, all the way back to Moses. His work with the Israelites back then is a testimony to his character now (v 7). He has been working in the world for a long time and continues to keep working.

> The LORD is merciful and gracious,
>   slow to anger and abounding in steadfast love.
> He will not always chide,
>   nor will he keep his anger forever. (v 8)

The God who revealed himself to Moses in Exodus 34 is the God of Psalm 103, and the God of right now. When we remember his ways, we see his character, and his character does not change. He is still merciful and gracious. He still doesn't deal with us according to our sins (v 10-13). And this gives us the resolve to trust him.

But it also shows us how desperately we need him. The more we meditate on who God is, the more we see who we are—not only in our sinfulness but also in our frailty. God might be unchanging, but we are not. Verses 13-14 form one of my favorite passages in all the psalms:

> As a father shows compassion to his children,
>   so the LORD shows compassion to those who fear him.
> For he knows our frame;
>   he remembers that we are dust.

God created us, so he knows us better than we know ourselves. He doesn't expect more of us than what is possible in our finiteness. He's compassionate. He knows how weak and uncertain we can be. Often, when we are confronted with our limitations, we can grow discouraged, but here David is saying that this is actually a comfort. Because of who God is, we can rest within our own limitations.

Do you want to know what God is like? asks David. *Look at a good father.* A good father understands the frailty of his child. He doesn't expect more of them than they are mentally and physically capable of giving. A good father has compassion on the frailty and limitations of his children. He pushes his 2-year-old in a stroller, rather than expecting them to walk all morning. He helps his young daughter make her breakfast because she can't handle the stove safely. Similarly, God is a Father who sees our frailty, our sinfulness, and our inability to save ourselves or care for ourselves—and he has compassion.

When we see God's character and work, it reminds us of how fleeting and frail we are:

> *As for man, his days are like grass;*
> *he flourishes like a flower of the field;*
> *for the wind passes over it, and it is gone,*
> *and its place knows it no more. (v 15-16)*

A meditation on our own frailty leads to praise not only for God's might and eternality but his love.

> *But the steadfast love of the LORD is from everlasting*
> *to everlasting on those who fear him,*
> *and his righteousness to children's children. (v 17)*

We will pass away, but God's love never passes away. Gratitude grows when we see God for who he is and see ourselves for who we are—he is infinite; we are finite.

PERSONAL GRATITUDE LEADS TO CORPORATE GRATITUDE

The psalm began with a call to personal gratitude. But in verse 20, the psalm takes a turn and makes the gratitude extend beyond ourselves, spilling over into the lives of others and all of creation. The benefits that God gives to his people—the salvation we receive through Christ, the healing we experience, the deliverance we receive, and every other benefit along the way—are never just given to us so that we would praise God in isolation. Our experience of gratitude is meant to be shared with everyone.

> *Bless the LORD, O you his angels,*
> *you mighty ones who do his word,*
> *obeying the voice of his word!*
> *Bless the LORD, all his hosts,*
> *his ministers, who do his will!*
> *Bless the LORD, all his works,*
> *in all places of his dominion.*
> *Bless the LORD, O my soul! (v 20-22)*

Notice the progression: David begins first by calling the angels to praise the Lord. They are the heavenly beings who obey his commands, who worship him, and who exist for him. He then calls the hosts (or the armies) to praise him. These are the ones who execute God's will for justice and righteousness. God is the Lord of hosts, the One who protects and orders all things by his power. He is the Lord of armies, the Lord of hosts, whose victory is already won and secure. Then David concludes this threefold progression by calling creation to worship as well. God is the Creator, and his creation sings his praise (Psalm 19 v 1; 24 v 1). Creation is full of his "benefits," as he rules and reigns over the world that he has made, and which is to live in obedient gratitude towards its Maker. He rules and reigns over it all.

This psalm builds in gratitude: first, for the personal ways in which God has dealt with David; then to the ways in which he displays his character in these benefits; then to all of the earth praising the Lord in gratitude. We should feel the bursting gratitude not only of David but also of the entire creation singing God's praise! When we live gratefully, we're living in line with creation.

Your gratitude is never to be expressed only in isolation. God's mercy towards you is not just for you. It's for all who come into contact with you. It's for everyone who knows your story and your struggles and your desires and your prayers, so that they would look at your life and say, "Praise the LORD. Praise him for the ways in which he never leaves her or forsakes her. Praise him for all that he has given and done for her, for all the ways that he's at work in her. He must be a God worthy of my trust."

This is not just a model found in the Psalms. It's a model found in the New Testament as well. Take a moment to read through Colossians 1 v 3-23, or Ephesians 2 v 4-7, or Romans 11 v 33-36. God's benefits to us are meant to be noticed, talked about, and shared.

Gratitude is a discipline best honed and expressed together. As we remind one another of the specific ways in which God has helped us, it leads to gratitude. It helps us not to forget; forgetting is what David warns us against in Psalm 103 v 2. We are naturally forgetful—and being spiritually forgetful makes us spiritually anemic. You can't praise the Lord in the way David does in Psalm 103 if you don't first intentionally remember all the ways in which this Lord has blessed you.

Are you specific in detailing to yourself, and telling to others, the ways that God has delivered you? When God answers the cry of your heart, do you thank him? God's character displayed in the Old Testament is the same character displayed towards you, his child. The work Christ accomplished on the cross is a benefit to you, his sister. God gives you the Holy Spirit to live in and transform you, and he will bring you all the way home to heaven. Every day you are the recipient of these life-changing and eternity-changing benefits. And you are the recipient of a thousand daily benefits from his hands, too, if you have eyes to see them. Do you recount all of his benefits? Are you filled with gratitude?

Everyone works through the discipline of recounting God's benefits differently, but for all of us it requires intentionality. We won't fall into gratitude. Maybe it means setting up a "wall of thankfulness" in your house, where you can place Post-It notes that recount what God has done this year. When I was in the hospital, and the year after, I journaled a list of the new mercies I experienced from God each day. It didn't take the fear or depression away, but it did lift my gaze towards God and help me cling to him in the darkness. We all have moments of thankfulness, but developing a discipline of consistently remembering God's gifts will bring us, and those around us, closer to God and more grateful for and to God.

For a small child, it is hard to remember on any given day the ways in which God has been kind to them. But it is hard for us as well sometimes. This is why we need Psalm 103— to remind us of how God has sustained us personally, how he has provided for us eternally, and how he has worked in the lives of many, many others. This leads us to greater faith in his ability to provide, greater hope for the future, and greater love of his compassionate character.

You have much to be grateful for, sister—and the greatest reason is Jesus. Forget not all his benefits to you. They are more than can be told.

Extra Psalms: Psalm 34, 98, 100

Journaling

IN NEED OF CONFIDENCE
PSALM 27

The LORD is my light and my salvation;
whom shall I fear?
The LORD is the stronghold of my life;
of whom shall I be afraid?

Psalm 27 v 1

As a child, I dreamed of making the cheerleading team. I practiced, I talked about it, I made preparations for tryouts. And in the security of my own bedroom, I felt sure that I had what it took to make the team.

But then I had to wait in line for my turn to stand before the judges.

All I could see were the other girls who clearly possessed more skill. Their jumps were higher. They had greater flexibility (which is saying little, since I have none). They were confident. Whatever shred of assurance I had in my chances of being an elementary school cheerleader disappeared as I watched each routine by my competitors.

I had no confidence.

My lack of confidence has only grown over the years. I see a faster runner than me and I feel no confidence in my running. I read a better writer or hear a better Bible teacher, and it leaves me with a vote of "no confidence" in myself. Let's not even get started on my confidence in mothering. I used to think that the more kids I had the more confident I would feel.

What is driving my lack of confidence? The ideal and the standard keep changing.

Cheerleading teams come and go, and so does the confidence that comes with making the team. Being the best writer, best runner, and best mother are all moving targets. If our confidence comes from comparison with those around us, there will almost always be someone better than us, which will undermine our confidence. Even when we win, it will feel shaky, not secure—because someone else may come along who is a better mom/teacher/runner/cheerleader than us. Our confidence will always be brittle at best, non-existent at worst.

Psalm 27 gives us a better kind of confidence—one that is anchored beginning and end in a fixed reality and not our own ability. This fixed reality changes how you pray and hope. It makes you feel confident. This is a psalm about a growing and sustaining confidence no matter what life throws your way. David gives us permission to feel the changing reality of life in a broken world and lay hold of the fixed reality of life with God.

A FIXED REALITY

David feels confident in verse 3 because of the fixed reality stated in verse 1. David's reason for trust is owed entirely to someone else, not himself. God is his light, salvation, and stronghold. God protects him both physically and spiritually. God is his fixed reality.

He needs this reality ever before him because of the trouble coming at him from every side. All throughout the second half of 1 Samuel, David is in a "stronghold" because of the threat of enemies (both outside and inside Israel).

His opponents were bigger, stronger, and richer than him. They should have crushed his confidence, and then crushed him. So the enemies in Psalm 27 v 2-3 are worthy of his fear—they seek to devour him, camp around him, and fight against him. It's a full-on war against David—but then something surprising happens.

Even then will I be confident. (v 3, NIV)

I would expect David to talk about his fear, especially when enemies are trying to kill him and are surrounding him on every side. But he is not unsettled in his fear. Instead the confidence only builds:

> *For in the day of trouble*
> *he will keep me safe in his dwelling;*
> *he will hide me in the shelter of his sacred tent*
> *and set me high upon a rock. (v 5, NIV)*

David expands his fixed reality here to move it beyond just protection. God cares for him. God keeps him safe in "his sacred tent." God doesn't just keep him safe among his enemies out in the wilderness, but brings him close and into his own house. All throughout 1 – 2 Samuel, it becomes clear that even though David keeps surprisingly escaping his enemies, it's really not a surprise because it is God keeping him all the way through, because God cares for him. Just listen to the words of 2 Samuel 17 v 14, where Absalom (David's rebellious son) chooses the counsel of Hushai (David's ally) over Ahithophel (David's enemy):

> *For the LORD had ordained to defeat the good counsel*
> *of Ahithophel, so that the LORD might bring harm*
> *upon Absalom.*

By all practical accounts, Ahithophel's advice to Absalom was good, though not necessarily moral. The only way to defeat David was to follow his advice. But God thwarted that "good" counsel of Ahithophel to defeat Absalom and to preserve David, his chosen king. God can defeat good counsel to protect his purposes. He is our stronghold. He is our light and salvation. He is a fixed reality for us. And he cares for us.

We can rejoice in this fixed reality even more this side of the cross. God was David's light, salvation, and stronghold, but in Christ these realities find their truest fulfillment and greatest expression. Christ is our light because he is the "light of the world" (John 8 v 12). Christ is our salvation because he was the perfect sacrifice for sin on the cross (Hebrews 7 v 27). Christ us our stronghold because he keeps us and sustains us all the way to glory. We should let this fixed reality of Christ's work, and our union with him sustain us as well. The Christ who is exalted over his enemies (Philippians 2 v 9) is our Christ. His exaltation is our exaltation. One day we will be glorified (Romans 8 v 28-30), and in the same way that our confidence is sustained by the fixed reality of our current salvation and protection, our future confidence is sustained by what Christ will do in us completely one day.

The Lord Jesus Christ is the same yesterday, today, and forever. He will care for us. That gives you confidence to face the day, whatever the day may hold.

TEACH ME TO PRAY

Once we have our hope set firmly on this fixed reality of who Jesus is and who Jesus is for us, then we learn how to pray in response to this hope. The fixed reality of verse 1 drives every single one of David's prayers in Psalm 27. He worships, prays, seeks God, and trusts.

> *One thing I ask from the LORD,*
> *this only do I seek:*

that I may dwell in the house of the LORD
all the days of my life,
to gaze on the beauty of the LORD
and to seek him in his temple. (v 4, NIV)

David asks for three things here:
1. To dwell in the house of the Lord all the days of his life
2. To gaze on the beauty of the Lord
3. To seek him in his temple

But it's not really about three things—it's about one thing. All of these three things are connected to his desire to dwell with God, who is his stronghold. As the war rages on around him, David doesn't first ask for deliverance from his enemies in this psalm (though he does do that in other psalms).,Instead, he asks to be where God is, to see God for who he is, and to be with God in his temple. And then he worships.

We can too.

Our desire for confidence should lead not just to a renewed trust, but a renewed desire to worship and be with God. And for us, it's even more accessible to us than it was in David's day. We can gaze on the beauty of the Lord through his word—it's as simple as pulling out your phone and using a Bible app. We can dwell in the house of the Lord with his people, the church. We are forever in the presence of the Lord through our union with Christ. Is this the one thing you desire when you sense your confidence waning? Even in his prayer, David sees that in seeking the Lord, he will grow in confidence (v 6).

Focusing on God through dwelling with him, gazing on him, and seeking him is what gives us confidence. When we know that God is with us, and that God delights in us, and that God is working in and through us, we don't live our lives constantly worrying about how we match up, and feeling crushed when we lose the comparison game. When our lives are shaped by the fixed reality of God and his love for us in Christ, we are no longer shaped by the unfixed reality of life in a broken world. We're loved by the only One who matters, and we're being used by the only One who matters. That's where our confidence comes from. We're not going to be afraid of others or afraid of failing if we know that God is our stronghold and if we desire him above everything else.

This doesn't mean ignoring the situation we are in. We don't pray and worship just as a distraction from our real-life fears and waiting. David himself prays for help in verses 7-12. His confidence in God doesn't distract him from his real situation, but it does give it a different perspective. His approach to his problems with confidence—a confidence in God, not in himself. So he is specific in his prayers:

Do not hide your face from me (v 9).

Do not reject me or forsake me (v 9).

Teach me your way, LORD (v 11).

Do not turn me over to the desire of my foes (v 12).

We can learn from David's pleas here. He doesn't shy away from honesty, and he doesn't get all of the answers to his pleas in this psalm. This is not a psalm of deliverance. It is one of trust. There is not a swift resolution. He is able to remain confident not because he has all of his prayers answered, but because God is unchanging and can be trusted with the outcome. I bet you don't have all the answers to your pleas either. I know I don't. I bet you a facing at least one apparently-insurmountable challenge in your life. I know I am. But David is telling us that to pray with confidence, and for specifics.

CONFIDENCE IN THE WAIT

The picture of confidence displayed all throughout this psalm is a confidence in something outside of David. It is God who is the deliverer. It is God who is the protector (v 5). It is God who exalts David after he delivers him (v 6). It is God who stands by him even when everyone else abandons him (v 10). It is God who teaches him (v 11). It is God who keeps him (v 13). And because of all of this, God is the One whom David remains confident in. God is worthy of the wait for full deliverance because God has proven himself time and again.

If I had had this confidence all those years ago while I waited for the results to be posted for the next cheerleader squad, maybe I wouldn't have been so crushed when my name wasn't on the list—again. If my confidence had been based on God's love for me and plans for me, and not on something as uncertain as the 5th-grade cheerleading squad, my response to not making the team would have looked very different. I could have worshiped instead of despaired. I could have trusted God and done my best, not worrying about the outcome. If I had desired the "one thing" of being with God instead of being on the team, I would have responded very differently to that situation, and would have had to find a different illustration for this chapter all these years later.

For most of us, it's not cheerleading selection that undermines our confidence. But it is something. There is a moment when each of us have to face something where we lack confidence in ourselves. For many of us, those moments come all the time, all throughout each day. And though it may not seem it, that is a good place to be in— because when we stop looking to ourselves, we're ready to look to God. When you need confidence but don't feel any, you need Psalm 27. Cry out to God, remember his beauty and his welcome of you, and find confidence in his presence.

The psalm doesn't end with resolution. But our lives aren't exactly all resolved yet either. In this sense, we are still waiting on the Lord (v 14). But that's why we need verse 1 every single day. As we wait, we can "be strong and take heart" because verse 1 is absolutely true for those of us in Christ. As we wait, we can pray with specific and honest words to our God, who hears our prayers and will not leave us. As we wait, we can seek the Lord in his house and in his word—in Jesus. And as we wait, we can remain confident that he will be our shelter from the battles that rage all around us and inside us.

If our confidence rested in our ability, we would be toast. But our confidence is resting on something that is certain. So be strong, sister. Let your heart take courage. The Lord is the stronghold of your life. You can be confident in him, even while the battle rages on, even when your flaws or your weaknesses are very evident to you. The Lord is your light, guiding your way; and your salvation, giving you life; and your stronghold, protecting you. There's nothing to fear, and every reason to live confident.

Extra Psalms: Psalms 9, 11, 17, 20

Journaling

ANGRY
PSALM 4

Be angry, and do not sin;
ponder in your own hearts on your beds,
and be silent.

Psalm 4 v 4

The red flashing numbers taunted me as I glanced at them for what seemed like the millionth time. 11:00 p.m... 12:30 a.m... 2:00 a.m... I knew sleep wasn't coming anytime soon, and my alarm would now go off long before I was ready to wake.

But I couldn't sleep. I couldn't stop rehearsing the fight in my head. I had said things I shouldn't have said. The other person had said things that shouldn't have been said. I felt guilty over my outburst of anger. But I was also hurt by what had happened. And I was afraid of what the morning would hold regarding this unresolved conflict.

I was still angry. And I was very awake.

Have you ever been so angry you couldn't sleep? Maybe your colleague treated you unfairly, or spoke harshly to you, or took credit for your hard work. So you tossed and turned all night knowing you needed to get past it, but also knowing that you just couldn't. Or your neighbor invaded your space but wouldn't admit it. They ruined your lawn or broke your fence, and you were left with the financial burden. You lay awake angry and overwhelmed by what might happen tomorrow. Maybe a friend betrayed you, spreading lies about you, and you knew the next day would hold more trouble than you could bear. You were angry over the injustice, so you couldn't sleep.

Psalm 4 is a psalm of lament, where David is facing attacks from flesh-and-blood enemies. There are psalms that deal with anger in different ways—including those that call down judgment on enemies—but this is a psalm where David fights to deal with his anger personally. Here, David is leading us not only to feel our anger rightly but to process it rightly as well.

WHEN IT'S RIGHT TO BE ANGRY

To put it simply, David is angry because wicked men are attacking him on every side. Instead of being honored as the king, he is being shamed. He is being lied about (v 2). He is being mocked (v 6).

Feeling anger over a lack of respect—over being the victim of lies or over being mocked—is not an experience unique to David. Part of living in broken world means we have people in our lives who really don't like us, and they take their disdain out on us through lying about us or mocking us. That's a hard burden to bear. It's also infuriating.

Christians are often encouraged not to be angry—to ignore or bottle up the feeling.

But to the question "Is it okay to be angry?" I think Psalm 4's answer is "yes"—if the anger is righteous. Righteous anger is anger over what God is angry about. God is angry about his name being mocked, his glory being stolen, and his world being mistreated. He is also angry when his image-bearers are abused, shamed, mistreated, and mocked—

when the people he created fail to honor one another, and instead abuse one another. The world, and all who dwell in it, is God's creation. So when the world groans over the effects of sin, God groans too. In David's case, he is righteously angry because he is being lied about, shamed, and mistreated. God is angry over such things as well.

Unrighteous anger is prompted when someone gets in the way of us securing our own glory. It is self-focused. But here, David is concerned about God and his glory. The attacks of his enemies seek to threaten God's promises and God's worship. Human beings were made to glorify God, so God's glory is directly affected when we experience the same sort of shame and mistreatment that David is enduring. And God is angered by it.

We see this most clearly not in David's anger but in our Savior's. All four Gospels tell us of how Jesus cleansed the temple of self-seeking people who were using God's house for their own gain. In John 2 v 17, as Jesus' disciples watched his actions, they "remembered that it was written, 'Zeal for your house will consume me.'" His anger was warranted. It was aimed at preserving God's name. He didn't shrink back from his anger at all; instead he used it with purpose. He let his righteous anger fuel courageous action—clearing his Father's house so that it could be returned to its original purpose: as a place for people of all backgrounds to come and meet with God without human-imposed restrictions.

We are often tempted to shrink back from any inkling of anger because we think all anger is sin; or because we fear that an outburst could lead to sin; or because we don't rightly understand how to use our zeal for good purposes. But the opposite of anger is not love—it is indifference. There is a time when the most loving response we can make towards a situation is righteous anger, and to act as if we feel nothing or to respond in indifference is actually the callous response. We are image-bearers of God, so in a fallen world we are meant to be angry over the things he hates. In his book *Good and Angry*, David Powlison calls God the "most famous angry person in history." Powlison says that when we look at God, we will see that there is...

> "... no one whose anger is so like your own and yet so refreshingly different. Remember that we were made in his image, with the potential for holy indignation at evil. And however twisted and upside-down our anger has become, the Lord lovingly intends to remake us into that very image."
>
> (*Good and Angry*, page 105)

So, when you feel angry, the first question to ask is "Why?" Is it because God's glory is being stolen or his image-bearers mistreated; or is it because the glory you wanted has been diminished or your desires not met?

DEAL WITH YOUR ANGER RIGHTLY

But, if our anger is righteous, then the question comes up: What do I do with that anger once I let myself feel it?

David tells us:

> Be angry, and do not sin;
> ponder in your own hearts on your beds, and be silent. (Psalm 4 v 4)

Even when our anger is rightly prompted, we then need to be careful that we are righteous in the way we handle it. This is David's point here. He is angry (and rightly so), but he needs to learn how to respond to that anger in a way that keeps him from sinning. In their book *The Cry of the Soul: How Our Emotions Reveal Our Deepest Questions About God*, Dan Allender and Tremper Longman compare righteous and unrighteous anger, particularly in how it is dealt with in the psalms. Using this verse, they say that righteous anger is an anger that waits and ponders:

> *"Anger should lead us into silent pondering rather than direct action. Usually anger is a starting gun that signals us to leap from the blocks to control, consume, and destroy. Instead anger should be a starting gun that calls us to sit down and think."*
>
> *(page 54)*

Righteous anger rightly dealt with leads to a peace that passes understanding. Unrighteous anger, or righteous anger unrighteously responded to, keeps us from sleeping.

Imagine a fight with someone, and the fault is theirs. Maybe it leads you to mentally compose a biting email, showing them who the real victor is. Maybe it leads you to re-run the fight in your imagination, where you always deliver the best lines of defense. Next thing you know, you are wide awake, unable to sleep. David is not telling us to bottle up our anger, but instead is giving us a guide for our anger. *Be angry*, he says. *The injustice against you is real. You can feel it and be angry over it. But don't sin.*

David says to wait, to ponder, to sit in silence. Why? Because that is how God acts in his anger. He is patient. He is gracious. He is merciful. He is long-suffering. Our first response to feeling angry, as Allender and Longman say, tends to be "a starting gun ... to control, consume, and destroy." We are tempted to consume and destroy the one who has wronged us—sometimes by confronting them in anger or by telling another person just how much that person has wronged us (thus consuming and destroying their reputation). God's first response is to wait and be patient (Exodus 34 v 6). He is slow to consume and destroy.

We aren't God, of course; and God's restraint comes from him knowing his own purposes and power to deal with his enemies. Our restraint is owing to something entirely outside of ourselves, which takes us to verses 1 and 3 of Psalm 4.

First, you need to let God's past faithfulness fuel your dependence on him in the present.

> *Answer me when I call, O God of my righteousness!*
> *You have given me relief when I was in distress.*
> *Be gracious to me and hear my prayer! (v 1)*

Dale Ralph Davis translates this as "in tight places you have made space for me" (*The Way of the Righteous in the Muck of Life*, page 49). David's basis for crying out to God in his distress is that when he was trapped by his enemies, God made space. If God can make tight spaces spacious for David, then surely he can be depended on in our distress too. As Christians, who each have a personal history of God's dealings with us (I'm sure you can remember ways he has made space for you in "tight spaces"), we too can depend on him in the present because of what he has done for us in the past. We look back to look forward. When you are pondering your anger and waiting to respond, the path towards not sinning in your anger involves remembering the ways God has gotten you out of tight spaces before. He delivered you before. He will deliver you again. You do not need to control the outcome. You do not need to win.

God can also be depended on because, in Christ, he has made us his own (v 3). He will not let us be lost or destroyed (Psalm 121 v 3). He will not let us be completely overtaken. He has dealt with our greatest enemy, sin, and will continue to make us more holy through the presence of the Holy Spirit in our lives. Knowing that he loves us and is for our good leads us to trust when we are wronged and are angry.

But as David knew, it sometimes takes a little bit of time to get to that point. So it is good to wait, pondering your anger in your own heart. That is not the same as passively ignoring your enemies. It is not the same as saying that the sin against you doesn't matter—it absolutely does. Your pondering is not a form of stewing in your anger, plotting ways to get even, fantasizing about revenge, or feeding the anger by recounting other sins done against you. Quietly pondering your anger gives you the space to hand over the situation, and the other person, to the infinitely more righteous God as the One who delivered you in the past through Christ and will deliver you again.

WORSHIP GOD AND GO TO SLEEP

As we depend on God and deal with our anger, we begin the process of moving to trust. Only then can we worship God rightly. This is the point that David reaches in Psalm 4 v 5:

> *Offer right sacrifices,*
> *and put your trust in the LORD.*

And, when we recommit ourselves to living for God in this particular situation that has caused our righteous anger, and we put our trust in him to deal with this situation, then there is another feeling we can enjoy that will slowly take the place of our anger:

> *You have put more joy in my heart*
> *than they have when their grain and wine abound.*
>
> *(v 7)*

David is contrasting God's joy with the joy of material possessions. By all accounts, his enemies have taken much from him, but God has restored his heart with more than any earthly possession can give him. God has given him joy. The progression of this psalm is towards hope for the Christian who is facing real injustice and righteous anger. Often we are angry when we have had something taken from us—our reputation, a possession, or an experience with a loved one.

But no one can rob us of our greatest reason for joy, which is God himself. David is saying that even when so much has been taken from him by his enemies, what God provides in the midst of it all far surpasses what has been lost. You can feel anger, you can depend on God, you can know that he cares for you, and then you can experience joy even when you are hard-pressed on every side. And you can find rest.

How do you sleep when you are angry? The fact that David was able to "lie down and sleep" was because he trusted in something outside of his own control. He trusted in God to make him safe, even though he faced enemies on all fronts, he was on the run, and he had men seeking to kill him—because, after all, verse 8 was still true.

You alone, LORD, make me dwell in safety.

Anger is a natural response to life in a broken world. We have real enemies. We experience real injustice. David tells us to "be angry and do not sin." It is possible. Jesus often had good reason to be angry, and he was not indifferent to suffering or sin—but in his anger, he never once sinned. So by all means, feel the depth of your anger over injustice, but then rest in the God who is sovereign over it all.

Sleep is the reminder that we are not God, and we depend upon his mercy and care. So we give the situation to God and we go to sleep. We've depended on him. We've recounted how he has delivered us in the past. We've dealt with our anger. We rest. And we wake up tomorrow to fight the same battles that threaten our peace, so that we can know joy.

Extra Psalms: Psalms 35, 94 (these psalms deal more with the psalmist's reason for anger, while Psalm 4 deals with his response in his anger. So these psalms are helpful in showing how to live out what Psalm 4 says to do in your anger in order to gain perspective.)

Journaling

_____
_____
_____
_____
_____
_____
_____
_____
_____
_____
_____
_____
_____
_____
_____
_____
_____
_____
_____
_____
_____
_____
_____

FORGIVEN
PSALM 32

Blessed is the one whose transgression
is forgiven.

Psalm 32 v 1

In John Bunyan's classic book, *The Pilgrim's Progress*, the hero, Christian, is weighed down by a burden he cannot remove on his own. He starts out on a journey to find the way to remove the burden—and arrives at the cross of Christ. As he comes upon the cross, his burden lifts and rolls off his back. He's free! It's a moving depiction of what countless Christians have experienced as they find their debt paid and their sins forgiven, and they are given the righteousness of Christ. Bunyan says:

> *"He looked therefore, and looked again, even till the springs that were in his head sent the waters down his cheeks. Now, as he stood looking and weeping, behold three Shining Ones came to him and saluted him, Thy sins be forgiven ... Then Christian gave three leaps for Joy, and went on singing." (page 36)*

As Christians, we are forgiven. It's an objective reality. The reality of our forgiveness is not based on how we feel but on our faith in Christ. And yet—that reality should affect our feelings. So, what do you feel about being forgiven? It tends to be that our main feeling is relief. But we should not feel only relief. Like Christian, we should feel like leaping for joy, and then go on singing. Or, to put it in the words of this psalm, feeling forgiven means we will "shout for joy" (v 11). Psalm 32 helps us fully appreciate what forgiveness means for us, and helps us to feel the full weight of how wonderful it is to be forgiven.

The bedrock of our faith is that our sins are forgiven in Christ. So this is a psalm that stands the test of time. It speaks to the condition that plagues us all—David, John Bunyan, Christian, you, and me. But it speaks to the forgiveness available as well. And it sings of the great joy that comes when you know you are forgiven in Christ.

YOU ARE FORGIVEN, YOU ARE BLESSED

The psalm begins with a prologue of sorts:

> *Blessed is the one whose transgression is forgiven,*
> *whose sin is covered.*
> *Blessed is the man against whom the Lord counts no*
> *iniquity,*
> *and in whose spirit there is no deceit. (v 1-2)*

To be blessed is to be happy. A lot of things can make us happy in this life—friends, family, jobs, stuff, food, hobbies, sports, and so on. But none of those things produce lasting happiness because all of them must end, one way or another. David is speaking of a lasting happiness that comes from being forgiven by God.

Every line in verses 1 and 2 speaks of the nature of sin. But every line speaks to a different aspect of sin. Your transgression is forgiven. Your sin is covered. God counts no iniquity against you, and there is no deceit in your spirit. Each word for sin here carries a different meaning—and taking these phrases together, it's clear that the blessing of forgiveness from God is that you can know that there is nothing left to be dealt with regarding your sin. It's finished. It's complete. It is forgiven in full.

Sin consumes us from the inside out, but God's forgiveness is deeper still. If your greatest problem has been dealt with, what do you feel? When you meditate on the ways that God has worked forgiveness in you, what do you feel? Do you feel blessed, like David does? One translation says, "Happy is the man whose transgression is forgiven." That is the response of the forgiven one—unending happiness. It's a lasting happiness. This makes us sing for joy, like Christian did when his burden fell off.

But I know that oftentimes I'm not singing for joy about this. So, how do we go to work on ourselves so that this is the way that we feel?

RELEASED FROM SIN'S WEIGHT

You start to feel the happiness of forgiveness as you grasp what you are saved *from*. David begins with a contrast:

> *For when I kept silent, my bones wasted away*
> *through my groaning all day long.*
> *For day and night your hand was heavy upon me;*
> *my strength was dried up as by the heat of summer.*
> *Selah. (v 3-4)*

The initial all-encompassing depiction of our forgiveness (v 1-2) leads right into this picture of a believer who is burdened by their sin, unable (or refusing) to confess, and overcome with guilt. In God's kindness, he makes sin weigh heavy on us because he wants us to feel our need of forgiveness. The only way to be truly free is to have the burden of sin lifted.

And so God makes it so that the reality of his sin keeps David up at night. It consumes him. He can't rest because the guilt is so heavy, so strong. Have you ever felt this way? You try to convince yourself that a sin you've committed is not that big of a deal. It is not hurting anyone. There are worse sins out there. God doesn't care that much. As you spend your nights trying to ignore it or excuse it, you lose sleep, so you are weak and unable to function during the day. Guilt nags away at you. Psalm 32 says there is only one way to be released from all of that:

> *I acknowledged my sin to you,*
> *and I did not cover my iniquity;*
> *I said, "I will confess my transgressions to the LORD,"*
> *and you forgave the iniquity of my sin. Selah. (v 5)*

Verses 1-2 are the emotional overflowing of what has happened in verse 5. Stop and think about the weight of verse 5 for a moment. Sometimes we miss it because we don't capture tone and passion just in reading a verse (as opposed to hearing it read). Maybe even read it out loud right now. "I said, 'I will confess my transgressions to the Lord' and you forgave the iniquity of my sin." David has spent verses 1-2 explaining the blessed life of the forgiven. He has spent verses 3-4 showing the heaviness of sin. And then, almost as if he's surprised or overwhelmed, he exclaims, *You forgave me! You released me from this heaviness. You brought me to the experience of verses 1-2.* Can you see the burden rolling off his back and the joy that comes from it? By the time we reach the end of verse 5, David is marveling at God's forgiveness. It's not just anyone who has forgiven him. His surprise and joy are directly linked to the fact that it is God who has forgiven him. That astounds him. It should astound us.

And now realize that David only knew in part the

wonder of forgiveness. He was completely forgiven, but he lived before the cross of Christ. By one sacrifice on the cross, the Son of God reconciled his people to himself (2 Corinthians 5 v 17-19; Hebrews 10 v 10-14). David was looking forward to that—but he saw only a shadow, not the details. We get to look backward—we know how God forgave us. God forgives because on the cross Christ paid it all. He covered all our iniquity by his own blood. Now God counts no iniquity against us because he laid all the punishment for sin on the Savior. He canceled the record of debt that stood against us (Colossians 2 v 14-15). Jesus carried our sins in his body on the tree, and by his work we are forgiven—healed (1 Peter 2 v 24).

We can sing the words of Psalm 32 with the same fervor as David—and in a sense with even greater wonder than David—because our sins are forgiven in full forever through Christ. "It is finished."

This is something we should never take for granted. When we look at Jesus on the cross, we see a glimpse of what happens when sin is given its full effect. It is a weight that eternally crushes, and we bore none of it. Hallelujah! Praise the Lord!

THE HAPPINESS OF SECURITY

Second, you feel the happiness of forgiveness if you appreciate what you are saved *for*. We are forgiven so that we can dwell secure.

> *Therefore let everyone who is godly*
> *offer prayer to you at a time when you may be*
> *found;*
> *surely in the rush of great waters,*
> *they shall not reach him.*
> *You are a hiding place for me;*

you preserve me from trouble;
you surround me with shouts of deliverance. Selah.
(v 6-7)

In the Bible, water is often a sign of judgment. In Genesis 6, Noah was saved from the flood waters while a rebellious world perished. In Exodus 14, the people of Israel walked on dry land while the Red Sea swallowed up the armies of Egypt. To survive the rush of great waters requires an act of God, and it only happens if you are his—and you are only his if your sins have been forgiven and you are in right relationship with him. And so David enjoys the truth that "the rush of great waters ... shall not reach" the forgiven believer.

Forgiveness tells me that the worst thing that could otherwise happen to me won't. I might lose relationships, jobs, status, financial security, and even my earthly life. But in the rush of great waters and in the day of trouble I stand secure.

Now I need to remember that. I spend a lot of time focused on everything except my eternal status. The problems of this life are just so immediate, so right in front of my face. Maybe you do, too. But whatever lies ahead of you today, you can live knowing you will be safe on that final day.

And not only that, but you can live secure when life feels like a "rush of great waters" right now. Perhaps you are staring at a busy semester, with very little margin for rest, and then you find out that a family member needs your long-term care for the month as well. When sleep is elusive and rest far from the horizon, the rush of great waters does feel as if it will swallow you up. Or maybe you and your husband just can't seem to get along. You have a brief pocket of growth and ease, only to face an onslaught of conflict, misunderstanding, and harsh words. There is no relief from these rushing waters. They are raging around your neck and on the verge of pulling you under—you feel out of breath and unable to cope.

Can Psalm 32 v 6-7 be true for you? You are not singing for joy. Your future preservation feels just too far off, when the trials of this life are right here, screaming that this is all there is—that there is no hope. Maybe you are living your worst nightmare right now. Is forgiveness enough to get you through?

It has to be. It will be. Because whatever you face today is not the worst thing that could happen—and that worst thing has already been erased from your future. On the day when the waters of judgment really would drag you under, you will stand forgiven, secure.

Water is often a sign of judgment, but water is also a sign of life and salvation. Jesus faced the judgment of God—so you will not. So the rush of great waters that laps around our heads, threatening to undo us, is simply a reminder that one day the waters will recede and we will reach the shore safely. As Christian says elsewhere in *The Pilgrim's Progress*, these trials are not a sign of God's absence but a reminder that he is taking us home to where the waters rage no more.

CONFESSION UNLOCKS JOY

The entry point into the kind of happiness that flows from forgiveness is of course, confession. If we refuse to confess, we lock ourselves out of forgiveness and its joys.

So David, having experienced the joy of forgiveness, now counsels others to do the same.

> *I will instruct you and teach you in the way you should go;*
> *I will counsel you with my eye upon you.*

Be not like a horse or a mule, without understanding,
which must be curbed with bit and bridle,
or it will not stay near you. (v 8-9)

So, confess your sin. The encouragement that David brings still rings true today. Don't be like a stubborn horse or mule that refuses to be controlled—that must be coerced into submission. Don't be like a stubborn woman who would rather let her body rot from guilt from the inside out than confess her sins to the almighty God. *Learn from me*, David essentially says: *Seek this forgiveness. Humble yourself before the mighty hand of God, cast yourself on his mercy, confess the horror of your sin, and find abundant forgiveness through God alone.*

The forgiven feel happy. They feel blessed, and not in some cliché Instagram form of "blessed," but in a deeply rooted happiness that can't be removed. The forgiven feel relieved and released from sin's heaviness. The forgiven feel secure. And the forgiven lead others to confess and to enjoy their forgiveness. They feel forgiveness that leads to life, transformation, and joy rather than a vague sense of relief, because they know what they have been saved from. They are relieved to the core, and they are joyful.

And so, as we get to the end of this psalm, we are ready to shout for joy along with David:

Be glad in the LORD, and rejoice, O righteous,
and shout for joy, all you upright in heart! (v 11)

You are forgiven. Think of what you are saved from. Think of what you are saved for. Think of what you are saved by. Then you can exalt, along with David, in the greatness of salvation (Psalm 21 v 1). Then you can leap for joy, along with Christian in *The Pilgrim's Progress*. Blessed is the woman whose transgression is forgiven. Blessed is the woman whose sin is covered. Blessed is the woman against whom the Lord counts no iniquity. Confess your sin and know this blessing. And shout for joy! For joy is how forgiveness feels.

Extra Psalms: Psalms 40, 65

Journaling

HOPEFUL
PSALM 84

My soul longs, yes, faints
for the courts of the Lord;
my heart and flesh sing for joy
to the living God.

Psalm 84 v 2

We all need hope. We need hope of more than what we currently have—for something better or different. Hope is what keeps us going in this life—it's what gets us out of bed in the morning.

Maybe you looked at the Contents page, saw this title, and turned here because you need some hope. Or maybe you turned here because you are feeling hopeful right now, but you want to make sure you feel that hope "Christianly."

The key to Christian hope is that every hope in this life is a glimmer of our greatest hope. You hope because you were made for something better than what you have right now, even if what you have right now is amazing. And the ache and longing you feel for more? It's God-given to make you hope for the best that is yet to come. (Jen Pollock Michel deals with this longing for home excellently in her book *Keeping Place: Reflections on the Meaning of Home.*)

HOPEFUL FOR HOME

We live far from my parents, and we make a planned trip every year to visit them. It's a long drive (as they live many states away), and the entire trip is filled with eager anticipation to be with them—to be at their house.

I know what is waiting for me at my parents' house: rest, fellowship, food, and uninterrupted time with them. I desire to be with my family. I love my family. I have years of history with them, so there is a lot of familiarity that makes me both long for them and feel comfortable with them. They have proven their love to me time and time again. I love being there.

But the hope I feel before a visit with them wanes as the visit goes on. Maybe someone gets sick, or we are all too tired to talk as much as I'd hoped. Maybe the time seems shorter than I thought it would. As much as I love our time together, it's never enough. I always want more.

That's the thing about our hopes in this world. The things we hope for, look forward to, and strive for tend to fade, or disappoint, or end. Including trips to my parents' home.

Psalm 84 is about a longing for home, but a home that we never have to leave. It's a psalm for the woman who knows God and the place where he dwells, and can't wait to get there. There are some who think this psalm was sung as God's people went on a pilgrimage to God's temple in Jerusalem.

But there is something important that we might miss if we don't see this psalm in its larger context in the entire book. Psalm 84 falls within Book Three of the psalms, and in this section crisis is the dominant theme (see W. Robert Godfrey, *Learning to Love the Psalms*, page 123). Many think the crisis which the people are facing in Book Three is the exile in Babylon—that these psalms were compiled specifically to encourage a people in exile. In addition, only one of the psalms in Book Three is attributed to David—it is as if the king is absent. And so Psalm 84 is a bright spot in a dark part of the Psalter. In many ways, up to this point we have dealt with some pretty dark stuff in this book as well. But here lands Psalm 84, with its deep longings for God, God's house, and the hope of restoration.

If you are feeling hopeful already, this psalm will show you how that fits into the greatest hope of all. But if, as was likely in the psalm's probable original context, you are feeling hope-less, it will remind you that there is a hope so great that it can never be taken from you.

THE HOPEFULNESS OF LONGING

There is unassailable happiness to be found in longing for God's house and knowing we will get there:

> *How lovely is your dwelling place,*
> *O LORD of hosts! (v 1)*

And then in verse 4, which with verse 1 frames the first section, the psalmist speaks of the One who dwells in that dwelling place:

> *Blessed are those who dwell in your house,*
> *ever singing your praise!*

God's place is hopeful because he is there. That is the main point, and every other point about God's place is subsidiary to the fact that God is present. His presence makes it lovely. God is a God of beauty, and the place he dwells in is the most beautiful of all. We tend to desire to be around beauty in this world, and that is a foretaste of the ultimate beauty that awaits us in God's house. Every beautiful thing we appreciate here should drive us towards worship of God, who is himself beautiful and the Creator of beauty.

So we long for God's home not just because of what it can do for us (make us see beauty) but because God himself is there. In the Old Testament, God's dwelling place was a big deal. In Genesis 1 – 2, God dwelled in the garden, with his creation. In the wilderness, God dwelled among his people in the tabernacle (Exodus 40 v 35; Numbers 9 v 15). In King Solomon's day, God dwelled among his people in the temple, which is likely what the psalmist has in mind here (1 Kings 8 v 10-12).

Now, reading this psalm as New Testament people, we know that God has dwelled among his people in a person, our Savior Jesus Christ (John 1 v 14), and that he dwells with us continually today by his Spirit. He has always been a God who delights to dwell among his people. And his people will delight to dwell, fully and finally, with him in his heavenly courts.

So the psalmist continues to list out the beauty of that dwelling place:

> *Even the sparrow finds a home,*
>   *and the swallow a nest for herself,*
>   *where she may lay her young,*
> *at your altars, O LORD of hosts,*
>   *my King and my God. (Psalm 84 v 3)*

God's dwelling place is not just beautiful; it is also always a source of good for his entire creation. The God who cares for such small things, like the sparrow and the swallow, is the God we should long to be with. The psalmist knows that God's place is one of refuge and rest. It's a good place, with a good God. He takes care of creation—so how much more will he watch over us (Matthew 6 v 26).

This wonderful place, and this glorious God, is where we are all headed if we are in Christ. And we get a taste of it each time we meet with Christ's people. That's because the temple now is—us!

Do you not know that you are God's temple and that
God's Spirit dwells in you? (1 Corinthians 3 v 16)

We taste heaven in our church family when we serve one another joyfully and sacrificially, knowing that in God's final dwelling place we will be working and serving in perfection and for his glory. We taste heaven in our church family when we enjoy fellowship around a meal, rejoice in our shared salvation in Christ, and encourage one another in the study of Scripture. These are the things we will be doing for all eternity. But the fullness is yet to come. We are forward-leaning people, hopeful people, because we know that however much this life gives us, or takes from us, our best days are always ahead of us (Revelation 21 v 3). When we have a good day among Christ's people in our church, it should make us long for more. It should spur us on to that final day, when it will be even better. And when things are hard now, it reminds us that the best is not here yet—we are waiting for that city to come.

HOPEFULNESS IN THE JOURNEY

The second section of the psalm speaks of a trip: a pilgrimage to God's house. The psalmist is not yet in God's house. That is why he longs for it and journeys towards it:

> *Blessed are those whose strength is in you,*
> *in whose heart are the highways to Zion.*
> *As they go through the Valley of Baca*
> *they make it a place of springs;*
> *the early rain also covers it with pools.*
> *They go from strength to strength;*
> *each one appears before God in Zion.*
> *O LORD God of hosts, hear my prayer;*
> *give ear, O God of Jacob! Selah. (Psalm 84 v 5-8)*

With the first mention of the "blessed" in verse 4, the psalmist spoke of the experience of being in God's house. But what if you're not there yet (which, if you're reading this, is you!)? Verse 5 is even more hopeful than verse 4 because it says you are blessed just by being on the journey to God's house. Just by virtue of your longing and hope, you find blessing.

The journey to the Jerusalem Temple wasn't necessarily an easy one. In verses 6-7, the psalmist speaks of going through the Valley of Baca, which isn't a known place, but the general idea here is that what is happening in this valley is not natural. This was clearly, by nature, a dry valley, and presumably not an easy place for pilgrims to walk through. But despite its dryness, the psalmist says that the pilgrims "make it a place of springs." How is this possible? If God is the source of your strength, then it can only multiply. If your strength is in God, then he can make even the driest desert valley a place of springs and pools for refreshment. Remember, the psalms are poetry, so the imagery in these verses might be speaking of literal rains filling up a dry desert valley, but it also might be speaking of a spiritual refreshment that comes when all external factors suggest you should be dried up.

So the strength of these pilgrims is in God, the God whose dwelling place is lovely and a source of good for his creation; and who multiplies their refreshment on their pilgrimage to Zion (v 6-7). Their strength is in God, who hears their prayers (v 8). They are not home yet, but they know they will be, and that changes their journey. They are hopeful.

Have you found similar strength and refreshment on your own pilgrim road? In all the difficulty we've talked about up to this point in the book, and all of the sorrow in the psalms, Psalm 84 gives hope. It's telling all who will listen,

You are just a pilgrim here. Keep going. You will be home some-day. And God will refresh you all along the way. The hopeful can keep going on the journey because they know the destination is sure and their strength is sufficient. We can keep going in hope.

THE HOPEFULNESS OF TRUST

The final section is anchored by the last verse:

> O LORD of hosts,
>   *blessed is the one who trusts in you! (v 12)*

Why are you hopeful? Why do you trust? Because of verses 9-11:

> *Behold our shield, O God;*
>   *look on the face of your anointed!*
> *For a day in your courts is better*
>   *than a thousand elsewhere.*
> *I would rather be a doorkeeper in the house of my*
>   *God*
>   *than dwell in the tents of wickedness.*
> *For the LORD God is a sun and shield;*
>   *the LORD bestows favor and honor.*
> *No good thing does he withhold*
>   *from those who walk uprightly.*

You can do a lot with a thousand days. Imagine three years full of blessings—family, friends, job satisfaction and promotion, a great church full of love and growth, a fantastic house, great vacations—and imagine those three years have no problems: no health issues, no money worries, no relational difficulties, no bereavements. Can you fathom that?

That is not as good as *one day* in heaven.

So when we catch a glimpse of that kind of life—a great day, or a year that just brings wonderful blessings—we're to think, "This is just a glimmer of a tiny fraction of what one day in heaven will be like." That keeps us hopeful in the good times. And it stops us living as though this is the best there can be, which brings with it the danger that we forget to keep walking forwards.

And when we see others enjoying all those things, and we're not and never will in this life, there's no need for hopelessness. Better is one day in our future home than a thousand wonderful ones here. Where you are going shapes your experience of the pilgrimage to get there, and in Psalm 84 the psalmist knows he is going somewhere amazing. So are we. Every other place pales in comparison with the place where God dwells.

If you are struggling for hope today, let Psalm 84 encourage you to look forward to God's house, where he dwells in perfection, and where you will one day dwell with him. This temporary home might feel like a permanent one, but it is passing away. Think about God's house; think about all that Christ did to prepare a place for you there, and long to be where he dwells. And if you find yourself brimming with hope today, praise God! May this shadow of a better reality spur you on. It's merely a glimpse of the wonder to come.

Psalm 84 gives us strength on our pilgrimage to God's place. It reorients our perspective as we make our way home. And it makes us hopeful. We have a lot to look forward to.

Extra Psalms: Psalms 48, 63, 128

Journaling

FULL OF WORSHIP
PSALM 145

The LORD is gracious and merciful,
slow to anger and abounding in
steadfast love.
The LORD is good to all,
and his mercy is over all that he has made.

Psalm 145 v 8-9

S ome days you just feel like worshiping. You step outside after a long day at work and are met with a bright blood-orange sunset draping over the sky—worship swells inside you. God answers your hopes for reconciliation with a friend—and you worship. The work project comes together by the deadline, against all rational expectations but in answer to a lot of prayer—you worship. There are some days when you just feel like living for God, singing to God, and thanking God for the many ways he has blessed you. God's constant kindness to us means that there are moments in our lives when worship does just come easy.

One of my favorite songs is based on one of my favorite psalms—Psalm 145. It is written and performed by Shane and Shane, and they begin the song with the words of verse 3:

"Great is the Lord, and greatly to be praised." Each line builds on the previous one, and as the lines build, their voices and the music reach a crescendo with a loud exclamation:

The LORD is gracious and slow to anger and rich in love, he is good to all.

I usually listen to this song when I feel worshipful. That makes sense because the psalms were intended for musical worship. Many of them carry the superscription "To the choirmaster." Psalm 145 is even called a "A Song of Praise."

All throughout this book (assuming you didn't turn to this chapter first!) we have seen psalms of lament, difficulty, sorrow, sin, and pain, but this is a psalm that is straight worship. And that is fitting, because as David gets to the end of his life (when many think he wrote the psalm), worship—despite all that he has walked through in his life—is all he has left in him.

Psalm 145 is for the days when you are seeing things clearly—when all you can do is worship because you can see what God has done and will do.

If we knew Hebrew, we would see that the psalm is divided according to the Hebrew alphabet, with each verse beginning with a letter from the alphabet. It required careful attention to write it in such a way that every verse matched the correct letter, but it also requires careful attention to read because psalms were often written in this way to aid memorization. This one is intended for us to meditate on. It is not only a psalm for that moment when we long to worship—it is a song to memorize and then recite to ourselves in those moments when we don't.

CAPTURE THE WORSHIPFUL FEELING

As David looks back on all that he has walked through and all that he has learned, it is striking that it is worship that comes to the forefront. And he is calling us to capture that feeling too.

> *I will extol you, my God and King,*
> *and bless your name forever and ever.*
> *Every day I will bless you*
> *and praise your name forever and ever*
> *Great is the LORD, and greatly to be praised,*
> *and his greatness is unsearchable. (v 1-3)*

As we have seen throughout the psalms, we won't always feel this measure of worshipfulness. So let's capture it! Let's store up and then remind ourselves what we know to be true about God, so when we struggle to see him and we don't feel like worshiping him, we have a history and backlog of his greatness displayed in our lives. Then, come rain as well as shine, we will be able to bless, exalt, and proclaim this God—the God who is gracious, merciful, slow to anger, abounding in love, and good to all (v 8-9).

And why?

Because he has done great things.

We get a beautiful picture of these great things in verses 14-20. This is the explanation of his character that is displayed in verses 8-9. David makes a long list of the ways God works in the world because he is capturing his reasons for worship. God's works display his character:

- He upholds the falling and raises up the low (v 14).
- He provides food (v 15).
- He opens wide his hand and satisfies the desires of every living thing (v 16).
- He is kind in all his works (v 17).
- He is near to all who call on him (v 18).
- He fulfills desires, and hears cries, and saves those who fear him (v 19).
- He preserves those who love him (v 20).

We can all make very specific lists of God's works for us, too, can't we? The money miraculously extends beyond the end of the month, when all your budgeting said it wouldn't. He gives you new mercies for the day, when at bedtime the night before the next day seemed impossible to face. He feeds a hungry single mother through the mercy ministry of a food bank. He makes his presence known to you when the day before it seemed that he was absent. He opens a barren womb, brings a prodigal child home, or restores a marriage. He makes crops grow. He provides rain when it's too hot or too dry. He keeps the faith of his children and brings them all the way home to glory. No matter where you are or what you have done, all who call to him in faith are heard by him and helped by him. He is as intimately involved in his creation in our day as he was in David's.

His character proclaimed in verses 8-9 is manifested in our lives through the big events and the small events—from the life-altering prayers answered in a moment of crisis to the cries for daily bread lifted up every single morning. God is good to all. It drives us to worship. And when we do, we should capture that feeling so we remember who this God is that we worship, and worship again tomorrow, and tomorrow, and tomorrow, whatever each day brings.

SHARE THE FEELING

As we talk about what God has done, we are also inviting others into that feeling. We are joining with the generations of faithful believers who can also commend his works to us and to all who will listen:

> *One generation shall commend your works to another,*
> *and shall declare your mighty acts.*
> *On the glorious splendor of your majesty,*
> *and on your wondrous works, I will meditate.*

They shall speak of the might of your awesome deeds,
and I will declare your greatness.
They shall pour forth the fame of your abundant
goodness
and shall sing aloud of your righteousness. (v 4-7)

David spends a fair amount of time capturing his worshipful feeling in this psalm, and here he tells us one reason
why. He wants to testify to those who are around him and
those who come after him of a God who can be trusted.
This God can be trusted, and his rule and reign will know
no end (v 13). As one generation sees him provide, answer
prayers, carry them through trial, and grow them in faith,
the ones watching in the wings are bolstered in their own
budding faith. "Yes, he can be trusted," they think.

This is a legacy of faith.

Our church does a women's retreat every year, and we
always include a time for testimonies of God's faithfulness
among our women. It's everyone's favorite part of the week-
end. We ask a couple of women in advance to think of the
ways God has been faithful to them and then to give that as
a testimony before our teaching time at the retreat. What we
have seen year after year is the fruit of verses 4-7. The testimonies of our women are deeply connected to the generations
that have gone before them. As they speak of God's works in
their life or the lives of their family, we are encouraged, and
it causes us to reflect on God's "wondrous works" in our life.
God's works are meant to be told, David says to us. They are
faith-stirring. They are strengthening. They are a back-and-
forth meditation on who God is and how he has personally
and intimately worked in the world he has made.

The key to worshiping God rightly is not found in meditating alone, but in meditating on his works and then sharing them with others.

God is a relational God who desires his creation and his people to speak of his goodness and to worship. If we don't join the chorus of the generations in worshiping God, his works will do it for us (v 10). He will get worship for himself in some way because he is the Creator of all things. Even his creation will cry out in praise. Psalm 145 is an extended meditation on who God is and how he works in the world with the sole purpose of drawing us all into further worship of him. Don't you want to be part of that joyous song of praise to him? You surely have much to worship him for. This God desires to be known because in knowing him we are truly living—we are truly worshiping.

In the same way, our Christian lives are to be a testimony to the next generation. As the children in our homes and in our churches see us praising God for his works, and even see those works displayed in their own lives, verse 4 is coming to fruition. Yes, we are the beneficiaries of a legacy of faith, but we are also the ones passing on that legacy through our service to Christ's church, through our regular display of repentance for sin and our trust in Christ's forgiveness, and through the many ways we talk about God's work in the world. When you meet with a younger woman, do you talk about God's works? In your homes, do you talk about God's works? In your Sunday-school classrooms and neighborhoods, do you talk about God's works? One generation commends the works of God to the next generation. We get to be part of that continuation of faith—and we worship God—as we pass on what we have experienced and been taught.

LIVE THE FEELING

This psalm is not just a meditation on why we worship. It's also a call to action.

The right response to David's final psalm is to sing the words of David:

> *My mouth will speak the praise of the LORD,*
> *and let all flesh bless his holy name forever and ever.*
>
> *(v 21)*

David begins this final verse by saying that his "mouth" will praise the Lord. We have seen that displayed all through this psalm already. David speaks of who God is and what he has done. But then David expands on that idea and calls "all flesh" to praise God too. One translation calls "every living thing" to praise the Lord. The creation that has been so cared for by its Creator is now called to direct its worship back to him. How does a bird worship? By making a nest for her eggs and caring for her baby birds. How does a tree worship? By bearing fruit in season. How does a woman worship? The woman who is saved by God, made new by the Spirit, and united to Christ worships God not only through singing in church but also in every good work her hand finds for her to do:

> *Therefore, brothers and sisters, in view of the mercies of God, I urge you to present your bodies as a living sacrifice, holy and pleasing to God; this is your true worship. (Romans 12 v 1, CSB)*

Your very body doing what God intended it to do through the variety of ways you work and enjoy God's world: that is a form of worship. As you enjoy the food that God provides for you, your taste buds drive you to worship. As you understand a passage of Scripture, your mind and intellect drive you to worship. As you deny yourself and serve a friend in need, your sacrifice is a way in which you worship the Savior who sacrificed infinitely more for you. As you obey him in your everyday, ordinary life, you are worshiping. God is looking for an all-encompassing worship, where every single crevice of his creation—and therefore every single crevice of our lives—sings his praises. Psalm 145 is inviting you into worship: by telling you to capture the feeling when you have it, to share the feeling with others, and to live it out in your daily life through all kinds of "living sacrifice" worship.

Some days we cannot wait to worship. Other days, it comes harder. But both on our better days and our worst ones, we can and must still worship. Let your worship be fueled by your knowledge of this gracious God, who is kind in all his ways. Speak of this God. Invite others into worship of this God. Shout for joy, sisters. He is good and faithful, and his mercy is over all that he has made.

Extra Psalms: Psalms 78, 96, 136

Journaling

FULL OF PRAISE
PSALM 150

Let everything that has breath
praise the LORD!

Psalm 150 v 6

When I started reading the psalms regularly, I was surprised by how long it took for them to get to praising the Lord. I knew the word "psalm" literally meant "praise," and my whole adult life I had heard how the psalms were the songbook and praise of Israel. But as I read the psalms, I saw a lot of other stuff that seemed to get in the way of praise—like grief, pain, betrayal, and lament. Praise came eventually, but sometimes it took a while to get there.

That's life, isn't it? Sometimes praise looks like hanging on—you declare that God is good even as the tears stream down your face. We have seen that in the psalms up to this point. But sometimes praise looks like what we expect—joyfully throwing our hands in the air and singing out praises to God. That is the feeling that is captured in this psalm. And as we will see, that is the feeling that we will one day experience daily when all things are made new and Christ returns to claim his own.

Psalm 150 is the final destination of every other psalm up to this point. It's the end goal for the Christian.

Let everything that has breath praise the LORD. (v 6)

It begins and ends with the call to "praise the Lord"—so let's get praising.

AT LONG LAST, WE PRAISE

Psalm 145 ended the psalms of David and also ended the psalms that have headings. Like Psalms 1 and 2, Psalms 146 – 150 do not have headings (author, audience, purpose, and so on). These psalms form a conclusion to the book. Psalms 1 and 2 prepare us for the blessed life and life under the king's rule. They tell us of the future in preparation for the difficult present. They give us a sure footing before the reality of life comes at us head on. Now, Psalms 146 – 150 usher us into unending praise. They tie everything together, telling us what the point of our lives has been all along—to praise the Lord for everything he does in this world he has made.

So if the word "psalm" literally means "praise," why take so long to get here? Part of it is that the psalms present us with real life. Sometimes circumstances are not tied up into a neat bow at the end of a long week, or month, or even a year. Your experience says one thing, while your Bible tells you another. The slow journey to this explosion of praise mimics the life that so many of us live.

THE FINAL FIVE

W. Robert Godfrey says these final five psalms "recapitulate the themes of the book of the psalter" (*Learning to Love the Psalms*, page 232).

In Psalm 146, we revisit the theme of being "blessed" or "happy." Psalm 1 tells us that the blessed one is the one who meditates on the word. Throughout the psalms we see further explanations of the blessed life. Here in Psalm 146, praising God for his works and trusting him above all else leads to the blessed, happy life.

In Psalm 147, we are called to praise God because he restores his people. The psalms repeatedly present the deliverance of his people by his mighty hand.

In Psalm 148, the entire creation praises God. This is an echo from Psalm 145, where everyone and everything praises God for his works, and Psalm 103, where recounting his benefits leads us to gratitude.

In Psalm 149, we praise God because he is the God who triumphs for his people. He wins. Psalm 2 tells us that the king will reign forever—Jesus wins. Psalm 149 tells us to praise him for it.

And in the last psalm of all, Psalm 150, it's just straight praise. Every single line begins with the phrase "Praise him." Psalm 150 takes the theme of various aspects of God's world praising him, and then calls us all to praise him.

We will praise in this way forever. We should be working towards it. We should desire it.

THE PRAISE OF PRAISES

The call to "praise the Lord" is a command, not a request. And while we are prone to seeing praise as isolated to enjoying worship songs in church, that is not the only way we praise the Lord—though it is one of them. Praise is often reduced to an experience: one that is contained in one place while the rest of our life is unaffected by it. But these final psalms give us the picture of a lifestyle. Praise is more than an event.

Psalm 150 deals with three questions:
• Where do we praise?
• Why do we praise?
• How do we praise?

First, where?

Praise God in his sanctuary;
praise him in his mighty heavens! (v 1b)

I used to teach toddler Sunday school, and one of the primary truths that we taught the children was that "God is everywhere." This is a really concrete lesson for small children because you can then drive it home by asking follow-up questions. "Is God at the playground?" "Is God in your room?" "Is God with you at school?" "Is God at Grandma's house?" It helps them to understand that while they cannot see God, he truly does draw near.

Verse 1 tells us where God is: both in the sanctuary and in the heavens. He dwells in such lowly places among his people and he dwells in his heavenly home. He is everywhere. In ancient Israel, his sanctuary was in the heart of the temple, but now God dwells among his people in the church (Ephesians 2 v 19-22). Through his Spirit, God is among his people when they gather and he is with his people individually. He is mighty in the heavens and personal among his people—that is, he is transcendent, and immanent. So we praise him.

Since praise is the point of the entire book of Psalms, then a psalm that ends with *Praise the Lord who is high and the God who is low* is absolutely fitting. It sets him apart from all other false gods who might dwell on high but never draw near—and from parts of this creation that we so often choose to worship because they are near, but which do not dwell on high. The God of heaven who draws near is the God who rules us and sustains us, understands us and helps us—and he is the God who is worthy of our praise.

Which brings us to the second question: why do we praise?

Praise him for his mighty deeds;
*   praise him according to his excellent greatness!*
                                        (Psalm 150 v 2)

In Psalm 145, the reason for worship was based on a direct meditation on God's nature. Here we praise the Lord because of the same thing. The NIV says we praise him for his "acts of power." And haven't we seen that displayed all throughout the psalms—as well as across the entire Bible, and in our very own lives? Time after time the psalmists recount God's history with his people, and here we are told that praise is the point of that retelling. Time after time we have seen him act in our own lives, and what do we do? We praise him. Praise him for how he saved you from your sins and gave you new life in Christ. But praise him also for the many additional ways in which he acts for you.

One of the great benefits of gathering as a body to both request prayer and pray together is that we can rejoice when our prayers are answered. If you stay with a church long enough, you will start to have a long list of God's "mighty deeds" to recount. But if you don't gather in "his sanctuary"—that is, with God's people—then you miss the telling and the hearing of the great things God has done. Answered prayers bolster our faith, but this only happens when we gather with God's people to pray and praise.

Now, in Psalm 150 v 3-5, we get to the "how" of praise. This is the longest section in this short psalm, and its length captures how our praise builds.

Praise him with trumpet sound;
*   praise him with lute and harp!*
Praise him with tambourine and dance;
*   praise him with strings and pipe!*
Praise him with sounding cymbals;
*   praise him with loud clashing cymbals!*

Every instrument plays a part in creating a beautiful symphony of praise to God.

But this is about more than just rallying the musicians to praise the Lord. Derek Kidner says we can draw the conclusion that we are to praise him with everything we have (*Kidner Classic Commentaries, Psalms 73 – 150*, page 528). Every type of instrument is represented here—the psalmist even issues a call to praise through dance. *Use what you have,* the psalmist says, *and praise the Lord.* No one is left out of this worship service.

The only prerequisite is a heart that has felt God's saving acts and can't wait to shout about the wonders of his works. For you, it might be using your voice to sing. It can be working the sound system at your church. It can be helping set-up the chairs on a Sunday morning, or giving financially with sacrifice and generosity so the instruments can be purchased. Just as Israel's praise of God was not limited just to the sanctuary, so the "how" of our praise is not limited simply to our musical capabilities (or lack of them). If we praise God everywhere and praise him with everything we have, then all of life becomes a sacrifice of praise to him. Your long days at the office are an opportunity to praise the Lord with all you have. Your time at the gym is an opportunity to praise the Lord with all you have. Your coffee with a new friend is an opportunity to praise the Lord with all you have. Your long hours working in your garden is an opportunity to praise the Lord with all you have. Even sleepless nights with a newborn baby are an opportunity to praise the Lord with all you have. *Use what you've have,* the psalmist says, *and praise the Lord.*

I think this is why we hear in the very next verse…

Let everything that has breath praise the Lord!
Praise the LORD! (v 6)

Did you notice the qualification for bringing praise to the Lord? You just have to be able to breathe! God created the world for his glory—"everything that has breath"—and the end goal for all of his creatures is praise.

All throughout this book, we have seen how our whole being feels life deeply, and now we arrive at the point of all of our feelings—to drive us to unceasing praise. Tim Keller says:

> "Every possible experience, if prayed to the God
> who is really there, is destined to end in praise.
> Confession leads to the joy of forgiveness. Laments
> lead to a deeper resting in him for our happiness. If
> we could praise God perfectly, we would love him
> completely and then our joy would be full. The
> new heavens and the new earth are perfect because
> everyone and everything is glorifying God fully and
> therefore enjoying him forever. So Psalm 150 gives
> us a glimpse of that unimaginable future."
>
> *(The Songs of Jesus, page 365)*

There is coming a day when everything that has breath will praise the Lord. Everything that has breath will bow the knee, whether under compulsion or in joyful commitment to his sovereign reign over all things. There is coming a day when the blessed life will be our life forever. God created us for a "Psalm 150" kind of life; though sometimes we live in the bleakness of Psalm 88 for a really long time, it is not forever. One day verse 6 will be true in complete perfection—everything that has breath will praise the Lord. One day we will see and hear and be part of what John saw in Revelation:

> Then I looked, and I heard around the throne and
> the living creatures and the elders the voice of many

angels, numbering myriads of myriads and thousands
of thousands, saying with a loud voice,

"Worthy is the Lamb who was slain,
  to receive power and wealth and wisdom and might
  and honor and glory and blessing!"

And I heard every creature in heaven and on earth
and under the earth and in the sea, and all that is in
them, saying,

"To him who sits on the throne and to the Lamb
  be blessing and honor and glory and might forever
  and ever!" (Revelation 5 v 11-13)

Sound familiar? Look back at Psalm 150 v 6—everything
that has breath has been made new and is praising the Lord
for his works, in every part of his creation, and for the great
things he has done. Our feelings won't be wiped away when
Jesus returns and makes all things new; they will be ampli-
fied and purified. We will feel as we were always intended to
feel—deeply and without sin.

It might take a long time to get there. But this is where
we are all headed, and this is what we anticipate and taste a
little of when we praise God together.

When we feel like praising, we need to gather with God's
people and bring what we have to praise him together. We
need to praise him for his saving acts and for his daily blessings. And that should spill over into how we live as God's
people throughout the week. Even if you are living in the
anxiety of Psalm 13 or the weariness of Psalms 42 – 43,
you can still recount what you know about God. You can
praise him anyway, because who God is never changes,
no matter how you or I feel about his dealings with us.
Praising God among his people recalibrates our hearts and
affections, lifting our gaze to the One who is worthy of our

praise. This is why the greatest display of faith for a Christian often is simply in gathering with God's people—in joy and in sorrow.

We end where we began—with the promises of Psalm 1 and 2. We will prosper and be blessed forever as we meditate on the word of God and love the Word made flesh, who is ruling and reigning right now. We will one day praise with everything we have in God's house forever. This is what gives us hope as we feel all sorts of things in the messy middle of life, and the messy middle of the Psalms.

Extra Psalms: Psalms 146, 147, 148, 149!

Journaling

BIBLIOGRAPHY

Dan B. Allender and Tremper Longman III, *The Cry of the Soul: How Our Deepest Emotions Reveal Our Deepest Questions About God* (NavPress, 1994)

Kristie Anyabwile (ed.), *His Testimonies My Heritage: Women of Color on the Word of God* (The Good Book Company, 2019)

John Bunyan, *The Pilgrim's Progress* (Banner of Truth, 1977 edition)

Dale Ralph Davis, *The Way of the Righteous in the Muck of Life: Psalms 1 – 12* (Christian Focus, 2016)

Dale Ralph Davis, *Slogging Along in the Paths of Righteousness: Psalms 13 –24* (Christian Focus, 2016)

Olivia Hunkin, *Dangerous Journey: The Story of Pilgrim's Progress* (Eerdmans, 1985)

Zora Neale Hurston, *Their Eyes Were Watching God* (Harper, 2006)

Transformed by Praise: The Purpose and Message of the Psalms (P&R, 2002)

Mark D. Futato, *Joy Comes in the Morning: Psalms for All Seasons* (P&R, 2004)

Mark D. Futato, *Interpreting the Psalms: An Exegetical Handbook* (Kregel, 2007)

W. Robert Godfrey, *Learning to Love the Psalms* (Reformation Trust, 2017)

James Johnston, *The Psalms: Rejoice the Lord is King, Volume 1, Psalms 1 to 41* (Crossway, 2015)

Timothy and Kathy Keller, *The Songs of Jesus: A Year of Daily Devotions in the Psalms* (Viking, 2015)

Kidner Classic Commentaries: Psalms 1 – 72 (IVP Academic, 2008)

Derek Kidner, *Kidner Classic Commentaries: Psalms 73 – 150* (IVP Academic, 2008)

Jen Pollock Michel, *Keeping Place: Reflections on the Meaning of Home* (IVP USA, 2017)

Mary K. Mohler, *Growing in Gratitude: Rediscovering the Joy of a Thankful Heart* (The Good Book Company, 2018)

David Murray, *Christians Get Depressed Too* (Reformation Heritage Books, 2010)

David Powlison, *Good and Angry: Redeeming Anger, Irritation, Complaining, and Bitterness* (New Growth Press, 2016)

Russ Ramsey, *Struck: One Christian's Reflections on Encountering Death* (IVP USA, 2017)

Richard Sibbes, *The Bruised Reed* (Banner of Truth, 1998 edition)

Charles H. Spurgeon, *The Treasury of David: Psalms 1 – 87, Volume 1*, (Thomas Nelson, 1996)

Charles H. Spurgeon, *The Treasury of David: Psalms 88 – 150, Volume 2*, (Thomas Nelson, 1996)

Mark Vroegop, *Dark Clouds, Deep Mercy: Discovering the Grace of Lament* (Crossway, 2019)

ACKNOWLEDGMENTS

Every time I write acknowledgments, I am reminded that a book doesn't wind up in a reader's hands without many unseen people working to steward a book project to completion. My name might be on the cover, but this book was only written with the help of a whole army of people behind me.

If Don Gates, my agent, hadn't encouraged me to believe that I actually could do another writing project, I am not sure I would have written the initial proposal, let alone the entire book. Thank you, Don, for so faithfully cheering me on in front of publishers and throughout the entire process.

Carl Laferton, Katy Morgan, and the entire team at The Good Book Company, it is a joy to work with you. Carl and Katy are the reason my words don't sound like stream-of-consciousness writing—they are wonderful editors. Joe Henegan and the marketing team are creative and joyful about spreading the message of this book to all who will listen. Thank you for believing in *Teach Me to Feel* and for believing in me as an author.

Writing is best done in community, and I am so thankful for a community of friends (both in real life and online) who help make my writing better. Kelsey Hency did an outstanding job of reading draft chapters and provided her keen editor's eye; these chapters are better because of you.

Laura Turner gave helpful feedback on anxiety for chapter 13. My friends, Miriam Poteet, Laura Breeding, Rachael Metcalf, and Kara Hilburn read through countless chapters and helped me see where I didn't make sense. As always, my brother and his wife, Zach and Emily Tarter, read for theological and biblical precision and for clarity. I am thankful for your friendship and your steady encouragement.

The women of Midtown Baptist Church, where I worship and serve, have had to listen to me talk about the Psalms for years now. I don't think I will stop, but I am thankful for their encouragement and willingness to listen to me as I somehow found a way to work the Psalms into nearly every conversation or every Bible study.

Two scholars whom I do not know personally and may never meet have been invaluable to me as I've grown to love the Psalms. Dale Ralph Davis, with his pastoral care and powerful preaching, has helped me not only know that I am not alone in the various trials I have walked through but also helped me see just how timely these ancient biblical poems are for our life today. As he says, they have really "gotten under my skin," and I'm not sure they will ever leave. Mark Futato helped me understand how the Psalms work together and how to interpret them. He also showed me that they are relevant for all of life—in the joy and in the pain. I am indebted to the labors of these teachers and look forward to one day worshiping with them around the throne of the King.

One of the questions I get asked as a mom of little kids is "How do you find time to write?" Like many mother-authors, I find time in the early mornings, during nap times, and on Saturdays. But I also find time because of a wonderful babysitter that my boys have come to love dearly. Thank you, Abby Senn, for caring for our boys so well—and for giving me the time to write!

My husband, Daniel, is the real reason you are holding this book in your hands (or reading it on your e-reader). He is the one who always gives me a nudge to pursue a project, finds time for me to write, and encourages me to keep going when I am tempted to quit. He listens to my thoughts as I work through a chapter. He believes in the work that I do as a writer. And he is my best friend. I am glad I get to live this life with you, babe. Thank you for freeing me up to write.

I dedicated this book to my sons because they were part of the valley I talk about in this book. They were too young to have language for it, but they felt it as much as we did. We memorized Psalm 1 this summer because as much as I love the Psalms for myself, I want them to love them even more. Thank you, boys, for encouraging me as I wrote this book. Thank you for being excited about the Psalms. I pray you would one day bow before King Jesus as worshipers around his throne.

the good book
COMPANY

BIBLICAL | RELEVANT | ACCESSIBLE

At The Good Book Company, we are dedicated to helping Christians and local churches grow. We believe that God's growth process always starts with hearing clearly what he has said to us through his timeless word—the Bible.

Ever since we opened our doors in 1991, we have been striving to produce Bible-based resources that bring glory to God. We have grown to become an international provider of user-friendly resources to the Christian community, with believers of all backgrounds and denominations using our books, Bible studies, devotionals, evangelistic resources, and DVD-based courses.

We want to equip ordinary Christians to live for Christ day by day, and churches to grow in their knowledge of God, their love for one another, and the effectiveness of their outreach.

Call us for a discussion of your needs or visit one of our local websites for more information on the resources and services we provide.

Your friends at The Good Book Company

thegoodbook.com | thegoodbook.co.uk
thegoodbook.com.au | thegoodbook.co.nz
thegoodbook.co.in